PTSD and the Undefeated Me

A Memoir

SHEILA KAY

FOR TAMMY,

THANK YOU FOR
SHARING AND CARING.
Your Sister in Him,

Sheila

FIRST EDITION

Names and locations have been changed to protect the privacy of individuals.

Web addresses cited in this book were live and working at the time of publication but may have changed.

Aristocrat Publishing (www.aristocratpublishing.com)
ISBN-978-0692480960
ISBN-978-0-692-48097-7

For publication permissions contact:
inquiries@aristocratpublishing.com

For "Doe-Doe"

CONTENTS

INTRODUCTION

It took several years for me to begin writing about what happened, even though on some level I was aware that I would be required to tell my tale someday. My first obstacle was the discomfort of the inevitable public exposure which would follow. I have always treasured my privacy. In fact, I can say a preference for confidentiality is a family trait that is generations old.

After I was diagnosed with Post Traumatic Stress Disorder, I shied away from the spotlight to an ever greater degree. Yet here I am, without regret or reservation. Obviously, writing this book was in the plan for my life all along.

Even after I was sure the time had come to write about the most tragic events imaginable, I was still tempted to make the book as happy and upbeat as possible. Rather than tell my story from all sides, I reasoned that readers would become discouraged or even shocked at some of the things which transpired, and what it took for me to reach this point in my life.

After several rewrites, I knew that it was neither reasonable nor fair to sacrifice the truth of the story in order to make it "pretty". In telling my story, I recognized the need for me be genuine, which meant inclusion of both the good and the unpleasant to the extent I felt comfortable.

The reality of life is that it is a series of ups, downs, and in-betweens. I concluded that I would let the story unfold, and allow readers to take what they need from these pages.

I hesitated initially out of concern for the reactions of others when I revealed my insufficiencies and the massive shift in my faith. Then I accepted the distinct possibility that the main purpose of the book is to serve others, not myself, making opinions about me irrelevant.

I also wondered whether it would be possible to write an autobiography that is personable and yet private at the same time. I was concerned whether the triumph in which I walk would be conveyed despite the tragic events contained in the book.

Endless questions continually circled my mind like buzzards around a dump site. The bottom line is that I may never get the answer to every question. My responsibility ends with writing what occurred.

One day I suddenly realized that the majority of my internal deliberations were caused by fear. It is the very same fear that has been my formidable foe since I can remember. Only it has grown larger and more vicious. This enemy is now more determined to destroy me and any gifts I have been given to offer.

It was then that I saw clearly I am ready to call upon all of the strength and courage I can muster to fight back. After all I have gone through in my life, I refuse to take a defeated stance again. Even more is at stake now than in my younger years, including my mortal life. I wanted to win in this battle, for however long and in whatever form that takes for me.

I became confident that I could write the book and that it would hit the mark on every target for which it was destined. Courage replaced fear with each sentence that I wrote.

The cathartic benefit of releasing my story is just one important reason I decided to record and share this chronicle. It is also my way of standing beside the courageous and generous men and women who take an active part in raising awareness of, and erasing, the stigmas associated with mental illness.

In recent years I have witnessed firsthand the faces of fear and confusion associated with mental illness and dysfunction. Sadly, there are people who fear or misunderstand us for any number of reasons. Far too many individuals who have mental health challenges tell no one. They may be afraid of accepting, and then telling, someone about their symptoms. I know, because I went through such a transition prior to my diagnoses.

Never in my wildest dreams could (or would) I have imagined I would experience a trauma of such magnitude or that my entire life would be altered. On the flip side, my mind could never have conceived that I would come out on the other side of it changed, but definitely a victor! I am a living testimony that each day you live, your chances of winning your battles increase.

No doubt, it is difficult to get back in the fight each time you fall. But the reward for doing so is life changing.

The descriptions and dialogues from my therapy sessions are excerpts and compilations from over several years. They do not represent the totality of my treatment plan or care. They are intended to shed light on my thoughts and feelings at certain times and to set the tone and nature of some of the conversations I had with my health professionals.

I included parts of my life that are not directly related to the events that lead to PTSD in order to provide some back story about me as a person. I could be a friend, neighbor, or family member; the unimaginable can happen to anyone. You may read something that is similar to your own life, or that reminds you of someone you know.

I want to recognize my amazing and supportive family who still accompany me on my voyage on a daily basis. They, along with God and His tender mercies, have enabled and inspired me to carry on with my head held high.

"There is no greater agony than bearing an untold story inside you."

— Maya Angelou, *I Know Why the Caged Bird Sings*

1 THE JIG IS UP: SOMETHING'S WRONG

September 27, 2011

A petite middle aged woman sits rigidly in a chair in a doctor's office in Marietta, Georgia. Her arms encircle her body tightly. The woman stares straight ahead, wide-eyed. She is shivering, not because the office is cold, but because she is frightened.

The woman is me, Sheila Kay. What follows is a memoir of my life. Within it are the reasons why I came to be here today.

—————

I have changed doctors recently and this is my first visit here. Right away I like this doctor because she is friendly and professional. We chat before she starts the examination and discover that we are both from Michigan. She asks questions to fill in the blanks of my medical and family history displayed on the computer screen on her desk. She confirms my medical conditions and the medications I take.

As I answer her inquiries I try to convince myself that the nurse who took my vitals a few minutes ago did not guess how terrified I am of being here. I don't want the doctor to know either. I attempt to keep a smile on my face.

It is important to me that I appear to be as normal inside as I look on the outside. I am dressed and groomed well and I speak coherently. I hope it doesn't show that my secrets have followed me here. I swallow back tears and answer her questions. My voice is low. I avoid her eyes. She verifies my address and phone number, then moves on to my personal information.

"And your husband's name is…" she starts as she runs her index finger down the computer screen. Before she can finish saying my husband's name, I completely fall apart. I scream, cry, and shake uncontrollably as I slide from the chair to the floor. The doctor is obviously alarmed and concerned.

She springs from her chair and comes around her desk to kneel in front of me.

"What's wrong?"

"My husband…is…dead!"

The words tear from my throat. Hearing his name stirs up ugly raw emotions. The doctor's office goes a foggy grey color. I can no longer see her in front of me because I am blinded by tears and memories.

Finally, I am able to tell her the terrible reality of how my husband died three months ago. I'm babbling and to my own ears, what I am saying is incoherent.

Somehow, she understands what I am trying to tell her. Tears form in the doctor's eyes when I tell her that my husband died from Toxic Epidermal Necrolysis.[1]

"I've heard of that condition, but never seen it in person," she admits.

She tells me how very sorry she is and that she will make sure my records are updated to reflect the death of my husband, William. Silently, I scold myself for putting on such a display, as if I can control my actions.

By now I'm inconsolable and rather out of control. *Stop it Sheila! You are acting crazy,* I reprimand myself. The doctor tries her best to calm me down. She even shares with me her own loss of a family member in the recent past.

I start to compose myself. I will myself to remain in the present day. The past few months have left me in a perpetual state of panic. I'm convinced danger surrounds me at all times. I need safety, even more than comfort, so badly right now.

We continue to talk and I give her some of the gruesome details which led to William's demise. Eventually she goes back in her chair.

"I'm not going to draw blood today. In the condition you are in, your numbers will be all over the place. You are definitely grieving, which is normal for what you've been through.

---

[1] Toxic Epidermal Necrolysis (TEN) is a rare, potentially life threatening immunological skin disorder in which 30 percent or more of the skin peels away from the body. It is most often caused by a severe reaction to certain medications.

You are also severely depressed." she tells me.

I'm thinking to myself: *Of course I'm grieving and depressed. My husband just died. Nothing unusual about that.* I forgive her for stating the obvious and watch her type comments into the computer. I'm breathing heavily but the room is not as hazy. I'm present but not here, which is normal for me these days. The doctor continues her appraisal.

"I'm seeing far more than grief. You are much more deeply affected by the trauma than you know."

I stare at her without blinking.

"Sheila, you need help to deal with this from a professional in the mental health field. I can make a referral if you want."

Something inside me jerks to attention at those words. I am clammy, dizzy, and a bit annoyed. I believe that my grief is normal. To not grieve or be depressed means I have forgotten him or didn't care about him. She should know that.

I'm starting to regret that I shared the circumstances of my husband's death with this woman. *How did I get in this predicament? Now she thinks I'm crazy.*

I continue to listen to her anyway without expressing what I am thinking. Intuition tells me that she has my best interests in mind. Still, I have no intention of getting the kind of 'help' she recommends.

But I do decide that she will be my new physician.

She performs a quick physical examination and we make an appointment for two weeks from now to get my blood work completed. I leave her office. I'm careful to keep my eyes to the floor.

I walk to my car. The air is warm with a slight breeze. I ache to get back home. The thought of returning to safety is my motivation to start the car. Lately, driving is next to impossible. I strongly dislike the task now; it takes monumental effort and lots of prayer for me to drive anywhere. Afterward, I am thoroughly depleted.

I avoid driving whenever I can. But today no one is available to chauffeur me to the doctor's appointment. Each time I do drive I congratulate myself.

On the fifteen mile ride home I wrestle with the main demon that haunts me, especially when I'm driving: the real fear of dying. I also reflect on the doctor's words in between my imaginations of an auto accident, car jacking, sudden heart attack, or one of any number of grim fates. I'm sure that the way I feel is quite ordinary.

I wonder what I said or did that betrayed my secrets and made her reach the conclusion that I was in need of mental health care. I really don't know the exact answers. But I know it all began on a day and time when I was forever changed.

2 HE'S GONE

Fifteen days into the nightmare which ended with my husband's death, I am on a cot in the ICU waiting room of a hospital in Atlanta. I awake from a fitful sleep. Morning is dawning. I can see daylight peeking through a narrow window above where I lay.

Two doctors come through the door. Slowly, I sit up. My back is stiff and my head hurts. For an instant my mind is foggy, I don't comprehend what is going on. Then the fog lifts. *He's gone*, I tell myself. The look on the face of my husband's doctor as he approaches confirms this truth without him speaking a word.

––––––––

The past twelve hours run through my mind like a short movie. Family, friends, and church members have gathered here to offer love and support throughout this vigil. Through the night we wait to see whether my sweet, most beloved husband will die or if God will perform a miracle and he will live.

As temporary inhabitants, we've converted this waiting room into an informal church as well as a living space. The room is full of chairs pushed together to create makeshift beds. Hospital staff provides pillows and blankets in which we wrap ourselves to fight the chill of the air conditioning.

Even though the room is a bit crowded, it is kept tidy

of Styrofoam cups, food containers, napkins and other debris common to hospital waiting rooms.

I feel only love and sympathy from each and every person here with me. They push past their own sadness and feelings of helplessness to make sure my every need is met. Supernatural strength puts a smile on my face as I quote bible scriptures and speak testimonies along with the others. We talk, laugh, read the bible, and pray all through the night.

Among my supporters are the father of my pastor and his wife. The older couple have been like surrogate parents to me in this fiery trial. My own parents are unable to travel from Michigan to be with me during this time.

The presence of the tall, elderly man of God gives me peace. He is calm and gives me wise counsel. He reminds me to hold on to the foundation of faith that my husband and I shared. I miss my own mother and father. I am blissfully ignorant my father will die six months from now.

My mother and older daughter, Kim, live in Michigan. They are brought up to speed by phone throughout the night. I talk with them a time or two. William's twin sister, Anita, lives in California. She also keeps in touch for updates through the long night. Kim and her husband Michael will be flying in tomorrow.

After a few hours of waiting I ask to speak with the doctor for an update of William's status. For some reason, I believe we are waiting to see if a particular medication will improve his condition. Several hours have passed, and now I feel the need to check to be sure this is what we are waiting for.

The doctor confers with me in the hallway. Trina, my youngest daughter and Sherry, my only sibling, are with me. I ask the doctor if we are waiting to see whether the new medication will improve William's condition. I am sadly mistaken.

The doctor informs me that he was instructed by his superior not to administer more medication to William. His condition is worsening. The doctor tells me that we are in 'wait and see' mode.

"We've done all we can do. If by some miracle he does live, we will most likely have to amputate his limbs. There has been severe damage caused by the amount of medication he's been given, which was necessary to try to raise his blood pressure."

He looks sad and has his hand on my shoulder as he continues to speak. As I listen, I stare unflinchingly into his eyes and blink slowly. I try to swallow but my throat is bone dry.

This doctor has cared for my husband since his admission ten days ago. I have grown to trust him and respect his professionalism and forthrightness. It was his voice I heard on the phone about twelve hours ago. His words to me were that my husband was "having a bad day and would have an even worse night." He has been here since this afternoon and through the night as he promised.

"He's blind now. His kidneys have failed and his liver is damaged. His heart has been affected. William's body is getting weak; he is not able to fight."

I'm totally numb. I ask the doctor to continue.

"He will suffer with a substantial number of debilitating and permanent medical problems from the massive skin loss if he does live. Although it's not likely that he will," he adds honestly.

Even as he speaks these grim words to me, his tired, swollen eyes are kind and full of compassion. I am aware that my daughter and sister have tightened their grip on my arms, one on either side of me. I feel the atmosphere in the hallway spin and compress, as if it has been swallowed in a vortex.

Then out of the blue, the doctor asks me whether I want my husband resuscitated if his heart stops. For an instant, I feel as though my own heart has stopped. His unexpected question has the effect of a physical blow.

Since William's admission to the hospital, I have been forced to make many of these types of grave, weighty decisions. Like this question, they usually come when I least expect them. I'm unprepared for the questions or the horrors of this whole situation.

Each time the questions come my way I endure a shockwave of terror. My constantly churning stomach turns completely over. Despite the love and concern of family and friends, no one can make the decisions on my behalf. I know I have to decide. Right on the spot.

When he was healthy, William adamantly refused to

discuss death, medical directives or anything dealing with either of us getting seriously ill or injured. As his next of kin, I must make these snap decisions based upon what I believe is best.

I am a take charge person who works well under pressure. These circumstances, however, are foreign to me and far beyond the scope of my imagination or abilities. The confusion, fear, and insecurity I feel while making these decisions have thrown me entirely off balance. My greatest agony is that I don't know if I'm making the right choices for William.

For many years, I have turned to him for sound advice and counsel when I am uncertain about a choice to make. Now he lies completely silent in a medically induced coma. My mind forms a picture of what is left of the strapping, kind and loving man I adored in a room just down the hall. My eyes automatically look to the right, towards the room where he lay among dozens of machines and tubes, his body in a state of total carnage.

I say no, do not resuscitate.

The doctor explains that most likely William's body has begun the process of dying, which can take several hours or more. At some point his heart will slow down, which will indicate that he will not recover on his own. He tells me they will let me know when he takes this turn and that I can be with him when he dies since I've decided not to resuscitate.

My legs weaken; Trina and Sherry lead me back into the circle of prayer and comfort. I tell the crowd of about fifteen people the latest news. We pray and encourage one another. I ask Trina and Sherry to give Kim, my mother, and Anita the latest news. Then I walk over to the cot and lie down.

Hours later, my band of loving supporters surround me as the doctors enter the room to deliver the news of his passing. Immediately, I am again peppered with a series of very important decisions. Do I want to see him? Do I want an autopsy? Which funeral home will pick him up?

I think that I look composed and accepting as I answer the God-awful questions on the spot. I actually feel a pitiful mixture of exhaustion, grief, loneliness and the worst kind of dread conceivable. As I voice my preferences to the doctor, I'm fully aware of the constant, low pitched noise that I have been hearing somewhere from within myself for about a week.

I do have the tiniest sense of relief that the suffering my husband has endured is over and he is with the Lord. I am released from the strain of talking to my husband and pretending he looks just fine so he will never know the extent of the indignity which ravished his body.

I am also relieved of the duty of protecting him from curious eyes and negative speaking in his presence. I no longer have to jump out of my skin when I hear the house phone or my cell phone ring.

Yet the price for these new freedoms is far too high. I would do all of those things for as long as it took if it meant he would live. All I want or need is to have him here with me. I refuse to believe he's really gone. This has got to just be some kind of test or trial which will soon conclude with a happy ending.

I am aware everyone is looking at me, which is something else I desperately want to end. I do not like to be the center of attention if I feel I'm being pitied. They are all concerned and sad - heartbroken for me. Everything and everyone is in slow motion.

And then just like that, this appalling phase is finished. It feels like a heavy door has slammed shut forever. The sad little group makes its way to the elevators. I can't speak or cry. I have the strange sensation of being in a silent and painful bubble which will surround me for years afterward. I'm among the group but separate from everyone else.

On this beautiful balmy morning in Georgia, I am ice cold inside and out. I remain that way the entire summer. When we reach the street outside of the hospital I see people going about their morning business. The little support group disperses; I'm certain there are hugs and words of love but I don't hear the expressions or feel the embraces. But the low sound from within me is audible.

My brother-in-law Logan leaves to get the car. My eyes are grainy and I squint at the bright sunlight. I look up at the tall building and my eyes rest upon a window that I perceive is William's hospital room. I imagine him lying all alone in the bed. I get the sense that the entire hospital is falling down on me.

I feel a huge wave of shock and every nerve in my body springs to life. I scream. Long and loud. I'm not in physical pain. The ache I feel is all consuming and inescapable. People are looking at me, stunned, as I repeatedly declare that I can't leave him.

Someone says, "You aren't leaving him. He's with the Lord."

I am familiar with this truth, but right now I really don't know if I believe in God or anything else. I try without success to keep from being placed in the car in this indescribable moment. My heart is shouting (at least I think it is my heart shouting and not my mouth) *HE WOULD NEVER LEAVE ME!*

On the drive home, Trina, Sherry, and I can't bear to look at one another. We are pitiful, dazed, and scared. I study the freeway signs intently for no reason at all. It is a very warm and sunny Father's Day Sunday morning.

As soon as I get home I send out a mass text to those who loved and prayed for us that William has gone to be with the Lord. I hope no one calls. No one does. I take out the trash and tell my next door neighbors that he didn't make it. I feel the sun on my back as I walk up the driveway to the house. My legs feel like wood, stiff and heavy.

It is still morning. I smell the magnolias on the huge tree in the front yard mixed with the scent of the tall pines which surround the property. The sights, sounds, and smells which once brought me such peace make me plain sick.

I go inside and lay on top of the covers of our bed. Trina goes to her bedroom, silent, then suddenly turns around and lies on the bed with me. Sorrow and confusion are etched on her young, tired face. She is asleep within minutes, at least as far as I can tell.

Sherry sits across the room in a chair, watching us. I've never seen her face look as it does now. She's trying to be supportive but I know that she has been through far too much in the past thirteen days.

We can't say much or even cry; we are just aware of each other's presence and the weight of what we've just been through. I doze off for a bit and when I awake, some time has passed. It is early afternoon.

"I know you need to get back to your family," I say to my weary sister.

She nods a reluctant yes. It is painful for me to look at her sadness and exhaustion. I lie back down and mercifully black out again and escape the awful nightmare through sleep.

The real truth is that the nightmare has by no means ended today. It has shifted and morphed into what will be an unknown deeper, darker, and more terrifying reality for me. I don't have even the slightest clue into what gear my mind has begun to slip.

3 RECENT WIDOW

It has been a couple of weeks since William was buried. Things have settled down to some degree. Kim and Michael have returned home. I will see them again in a few weeks. Anita went back to California the evening of the funeral. I have decided to move out of the house. I've started packing already. I have no idea where I will take up residence. The state of Georgia has lost every bit of its southern charm to me. Maybe I'll leave the state.

Time has not been kind to me since William's death, although the people who care about me have been amazingly loving and loyal. Church members still offer to bring food to the house. Trina and I don't have much of an appetite. Sherry, Logan, and my nieces keep check on us. My mother calls to see how I'm doing. Everyone is desperate to do something – anything –to help.

I feel worse as the weeks go by. I am obsessed with keeping track of the time since William died. I monitor how many days, hours, and minutes ago he was alive. For instance, I'll take note of the day or time and say to myself that he was alive at the same time a month ago. Or I'll deliberately recall the last Tuesday, for example, that he was here with me. I try to stop the gruesome habit without success.

Immediately following the funeral I plunge ahead attending church and all related activities. Within a couple of months it becomes far too difficult to interact with the same people who had served God with my husband and me.

The sights, sounds, and smell of the church itself make me ill and miserable. Even driving in the same neighborhood as the church is painful for me, especially since the funeral home is next door to the church.

Eventually, I stop attending our former church and avoid contact with church members. I have only enough energy to concentrate on staying alive through each day of awful loneliness. Odd thoughts and behaviors are becoming troublesome. As strange as they are, at this point I'm confident that my thinking and actions are typical for a grieving widow of fifty two.

Some days I stand fully clothed for hours, without the water running, in the back corner of the shower where the wall curves inward. I feel cocooned, as if William's arms are around me. One afternoon I stand there with my eyes closed, crying and babbling. I do not know how long I have been there until I hear Trina's voice.

"Mom?" She sounds alarmed.

I open my eyes and see her standing outside of the shower. The look of sadness and confusion on her face shattered the few shards of my heart that remain today.

"Are you ok?" She turns on the light and reaches out her hand to help me out of the shower.

"Come on out of here."

"I'm ok," I tell her. "I'm just a little sad right now."

I feel embarrassed and a little silly for talking to her like she is a child. *Just a little sad right now? Really Sheila?* She's twenty two years old and well aware things are more than a little sad.

Trina is going through such a hard time. Every day I grieve for her loss of happiness. She tries her best to comfort and support me while trying to process the horror of what happened. Trina is worried about me. I feel I failed her because I am unable to save her from all of this. But I make sure I do not stay in the shower past noon any more, long before she returns home from work.

I deliberately refrain from talking to my dead husband, even though he was my constant companion and a terrific listener. I've heard stories of widows and widowers who set dinner tables for two and talk to their deceased spouses. I feel so sorry for them.

I have moved out of the home we shared together. I grew to detest it completely. The sudden detachment from William turns me into a walking, breathing, ragged gaping wound of a human being. I no longer feel I am a woman. What's worse sometimes is that I look perfectly normal.

I wake each morning and for the first thirty seconds I am blessedly ignorant. Then my appalling reality pours into my mind and heart. It is a feeling far worse than what I imagine death will be. I spend an hour or so thinking of reasons why I should not end this abysmal misery. Without exception, the main reason is because of the intense pain it will inflict upon those who love me.

Family members visit frequently these dark days.

Other times I go to visit them and we try to socialize as we always have over the years. They all try to keep up a brave front for my sake as they experience their own grief and sorrow over what has happened to someone they loved very much.

They try not to let on that they see I am not the same person. Although they do their best to conceal them, the expressions on their faces at times let me know when I'm being "weird", as I call it. For me, this is my cue to leave and be alone, not because I am unwelcome but because I don't want to spoil our time together.

Sometimes I can't help but talk about what happened to William. Even as the words spill from my lips I realize how awful it must be for them to hear what I am saying. I appreciate that they sacrifice their own pleasant family time to allow me to express myself.

Then I feel guilt and regret for spoiling the happy day they are trying to have. Many nights I lay in bed unable to sleep because I hear the echoes of my voice speaking the unspeakable. I see their smiles slide away and I know I'm the reason.

My daughters and son-in-law inspire me to stay alive simply because they exist. I know how much they love me and that we need each other. They know how much I love them but they don't know they are the only reason I decide to live.

Ultimately, I am alone in what I really think and feel behind my smiles, make-up, and nice clothing. Well, there's also the low hum inside of me that is my constant companion. I make a weak attempt at being the nurturing matriarch of what is left of my family. Beneath it all, anger sits right beside grief at a low simmer. He left me here, suddenly. It's not fair.

William was my husband. I am still his wife despite his death. Therefore, it is my duty alone to keep his memory and what happened to him alive for as long as I live. I am the official keeper of his remembrance.

I have endless conversations with Sherry about my thoughts and fears.

"I feel that I failed him Sherry," I tell her one day.

"How could you have done any more for him, Sheila? God knew that William would not have survived here in the condition that he was left in. It was His call, not ours."

I take comfort in what she and others tell me to help me cope. Although it is hard, I try to recall their words and hold on to them in my unbearable moments. Sometimes I'm in his hospital room and recite each of our conversations, verbatim, during the last thirteen days of his life. I see every detail in his devastated face and body as he tries to reward me with a weak smile when I enter his room.

Then I am there, trying to feed him before he was placed in the coma. I see his bandaged hand hit the white bed sheet, impatiently, when he gets tired of me forcing him to eat. Like watching a movie, I view my laughter at that moment. I told myself he was getting well, coming back to himself. I'm there in that room, over and over again.

Should I be repeatedly revisiting that miserable scene? It's like I'm right there. Am I daydreaming? At first I think these scenes are just bad memories, but I get concerned when I cannot shake them off. They become more intense. Maybe as time passes, they won't be so vivid.

———

Leaving my house is a necessary evil, though I avoid it when I can. As the days go by I venture out of the house as I am willing and able, mostly to get supplies and food.

I survive by developing routines which I stick to religiously. They give me something to hold on to. I am proud that I have a routine down pat. First, I carefully plan ahead which errands I will run, including the route I will take and what music I will play (and in what order) in the car.

Once I am dressed, I look out of the window to see if anyone is outside. If so, I stand just inside the doorway until the coast is clear. Then I step onto the porch. Before I pull the door shut and lock it, I study my hands very intently to ensure that my keys are really in my hand and not in the house.

I sit in the car and wait until my hands stop shaking and my heart slows and then I drive away very carefully. On a good day I am able to complete my tasks. Other days I leave groceries in shopping carts or prescriptions remain with the pharmacist until I can try again when I'm not so bone tired or frightened.

To the casual observer on the street I am a well dressed, perhaps shy, middle aged woman going about her day. But as the days go on, if my mind stops racing for a few moments, I see curious patterns developing. I don't see them as disturbing or harmful right now but sometimes they do make me wonder.

Some days are so unbearable that I question why I was born.

4 THE EARLY MOTOWN YEARS

I am born on a cold winter morning in Detroit, Michigan during the height of the Civil Rights Movement. I'm a preschooler when I notice grownups speaking in serious, hushed tones about a man called "President Kennedy" and a "Cuban Missile Crisis".

Not long afterward, I watch people on television crying when the missile crisis man is shot in the head and dies. So I cry too, but not because I understand what it all means. It's just that I really dislike it when things seem to be is wrong, whether it is in my house or out in the world.

Time moves on and now I am a young girl. My mother, sister, teachers and friends make up my world. The "Motown Sound" is the soundtrack of my childhood; its soulful sounds fill the air on the humble streets I'm being raised. The Temptations, Diana Ross and the Supremes, Smokey Robinson...all the music greats are like friends to Detroit residents.

The kids mimic their parents singing and dancing to the world famous smooth tempos and upbeats. I enjoy the singing and dancing but don't realize until many years later that, although I do have a measure of musical talent, I am more gifted in the areas of business and writing. This is probably why I begin reading long before I start school.

Like most youngsters, Sherry and I kill time after school and weekends with activities like watching television, listening to music, and going to the movies.

Summer days are filled with outdoor childhood games like "two square", jump rope, bike riding, and group games such as "Mother May I?" and dodge ball. Kids never measure each other in terms of rich or poor. All of the children just share whatever they have to play with or make up games.

I have a sweet smile, so I'm told. I have thick brown hair, big brown eyes, and a big heart. I am a super-sensitive child and very shy. I wear cat-eye glasses because of a weak left eye - this doesn't help my timidity. Like all children, I am teased for my differences which include being "cross-eyed", skinny, tiny, and smart.

My sister Sherry and I share a love of reading, like our mother. Sherry reads to me when I'm too young to make out bigger words, like when I try to make out the words in my mother's copies of *Man in the Grey Flannel Suit* and *Mad Magazine*.

I'm addicted to reading and not ashamed of it. When I am about seven years old, my mother brings me home from an eye doctor appointment. My eyes are blurry from the eye drops that were used to dilate my pupils. I am desperate to get home to read. When I get there, I'm frustrated to tears when I can't make out the words in the *TV Guide*.

It is more common to find me under a tree reading a book than playing sports; unlike my sister, who does both equally well. The books and magazines we read take us away to interesting places. We become part of the exciting adventures that jump from the pages.

Our copies of *Archie* and *Superman* comic books are worn and falling apart because we read and re-read them so much. Some of the favorite books we share together are *The Moffats* by Eleanor Estes, *Mr. Popper's Penguins* by Richard Atwater and Florence Atwater and, later, *The Bride Wore Braids* by Frederick Laing.

Sherry and I get involved with each of the characters in the books we share. We imagine ourselves as part of the Moffat family or gathering ice for Mr. Popper to keep the penguins cool. When we're older, we shutter at the thought of having to get married young because of an unplanned pregnancy, like the young bride and her husband.

During the school year I consistently stay in the school's library (even skipping lunch sometimes) immersed in my reading preferences which are fiction, poetry and "self help" books, as they will be called in the future.

I am now about nine years old and have taken an interest in etiquette and beauty. *The Leslie Uggams Beauty Book* and beauty magazines are my "bibles" on how to look, talk, sit, and dress.

I'm hopeful that one day I might be as cool, collected, and lovely as the women on the pages. I very much enjoy looking at the clothes and hairstyles, I even practice how they sit and try to imitate their facial expressions…always in private.

Every other Tuesday, the Bookmobile comes to my neighborhood. The mobile library bus is small and filled with the scent of books, which brings content and happy feelings inside me. I look forward to this exciting event in which I get to choose two books from the packed shelves. I am allowed to keep them for two whole weeks. Even in the dead of a Michigan winter, I smile as I walk around the corner to where the bus is parked for two hours in the late afternoon on streets filled with ice and snow.

———

My mother and her friend came to pick me up from school early today. As we walked home I saw some kids burning a flag on the ground. My mother kept me close and said something to her girlfriend about them "getting ready to tear this place up". I will put her comment out of my mind since school will be out for the summer soon. If those bad kids tear the school up, the grownups can rebuild it by the time schools starts again in the fall.

It is a few weeks later. Detroit has made world news as the race riots of the summer of 1967 destroy its streets. I have no idea what race riot means. I don't understand why people would set fires because they lost a race. But I know my mother will have the answer, as always.

I finally get up the nerve to ask.

"Why are they mad just because they loss the race, Mama?"

"No, it has nothing to do with a race like a game. Negroes are mad because of how they are being treated by White people," she answers.

Up until now I really have not comprehended that we

are treated differently. In the poor section of the city we are equal as far as my eight-year-old eyes can see. I have White friends that I play with regularly. I see White people in stores and other places. Our landlord is White. But I trust what my mother said, and start watching for signs of its truthfulness.

I am so scared of the big army tanks I see when we drive down the street. It does not take me long to become aware that people are treated differently, now that I have begun to take notice. I have not experienced any major disparity, but I've noticed White people being served ahead of us sometimes. And I did hear a White lady call me a "little nigger" one time.

I am sad that they burned up the stores because the city looks so ugly. Deep down I am scared too; it is no secret that I am a very sensitive child. Some of my strengths lie in my ability to comprehend, accept, and adjust to adversity. I am loved and I am smart. So I just keep reading, do my best to avoid conflict, and try to be a good girl.

————

Yesterday, my mother told me to go downstairs and tell her neighbor friend "that man died". I'm sick to my stomach because I know it is the man I have been seeing on television, Dr. Martin Luther King, Jr. I saw him on television a whole lot. I think he was so smart and his wife is so pretty. In school we are learning some of his speeches and songs they sing during marches.

I, like most everyone, am upset about the shooting,

especially since I do know the main reason it happened. For a long time I think I'm going to get shot too, because my skin color is the same as his complexion. My mother and sister's complexions are light so they should be safe.

They start talking about Dr. King a lot at school and I get even more of an understanding why he was killed. I begin to feel anxious about the world, like all children when they grasp that the world can be a not so nice place.

Soon after, another man is shot dead. He is White, the brother of the president who got killed when I was little. I walk around feeling weird because the world seems to be going bad just as my favorite part of the year is in full bloom. The grass is bright green and the new leaves are on the trees. I don't understand why everything can't be happy.

I do not like the fact that I take so much to heart. I see it as a weakness since I don't know the meanings of the words compassion and sympathy, which are inherent to my character. I despise arguments and fights; I have difficulty defending myself.

Almost fifty years from now, I will learn that extreme shyness, insecurity, sensitivity, and family issues can possibly result in susceptibility to Post Traumatic Stress Disorder, or other conditions, in the event of a major trauma.

In the meantime, I escape in my books. Now other kids are starting to like me because I'm smart. They ask for help with schoolwork and say they wish they were smart like me.

My mother and big sister are the only people in this world I love. With the exception of my stepfather, they are the only people that I really trust outside of a few of my teachers. At the age of ten I meet a first cousin for the first time and grow to love her dearly.

I do have a few girlfriends who I enjoy being with sometimes. Some of them are starting to like boys. I don't give boys a sustained thought except, of course, Michael Jackson.

With few exceptions, I am afraid and bashful around people I don't know. I don't have the nice clothes and accessories, and shoes, or other things that I believe make girls pretty. I am mortified when I am on an overnight visit at a friend of my mother's with a bunch of other kids and the lady points out that a boy that is there likes me.

But I do know I have the power to persuade people to make peace and that I am not afraid of trying new things. I'm creative, funny, and intuitive.

Sherry is the only person that I share everything about myself with. Together, we survive the ups and downs of the streets of Detroit, school, family issues, being poor, and simply growing up. She is four years older and bossy like all older siblings.

My mother mandates that she watch out for me as the younger, smaller, more sensitive child. Sherry is fiercely protective of me. Her defensiveness will last long after we grow up. It will spread to her husband, children, and grandchildren when she is the matriarch of her own family.

As the oldest, Sherry baby-sits me when my mother is at work or out with friends. She is entertaining and hilariously funny. We play games, watch television and read to keep occupied when we are home alone.

Her bossiness gets on my nerves, but usually by that time I'm sleepy or my mother returns. I won't comprehend the difficulty she had being responsible for me sometimes until I am much older. I guess that's what it is like being the oldest child.

I am finally a teenager. We are Jehovah's Witnesses. Our family is accepted into the tight knit religious community. I am enjoying all of the fun outings like house parties, roller skating, wedding receptions and other entertainment that Jehovah's Witness teenagers do together regularly. I have lots of friends and I fit in just fine.

However, I have an overwhelming fear of Jehovah God as defined by the Witnesses. I envision him as a dark grey colored angry Being, always frowning. He's displeased because I am unable to keep each and every one of his commandments as outlined in the bible, especially the Old Testament. As such, I don't expect to be accepted into Jehovah's "new world" after the "battle of Armageddon". But in the meantime I enjoy the perks of belonging to a group of people who think and act like me.

I am not the ugly duckling I thought I was all these years. Several boys are attracted to me and my sister, despite the fact that we don't have the nice clothes that a lot of the things girls our age possess. But our mother has instilled in us to be neat and clean and behave like ladies. Sometimes I am jealous of the young people that have more than I do. I don't let it affect my friendships, though.

I'm taking an interest in the opposite sex now but they are not my main priority, yet. My full life now consists of school, social and family activities, and attending and participating in the Kingdom Hall (their version of church) activities five times each week.

I have no aspirations in life other than to serve Jehovah (God) and maybe be a good wife one day. It is the 1970's, when Jehovah's Witnesses are discouraged from achieving success outside of serving within the religion, such as going door to door offering literature and participating in meetings which teach congregants how to approach and convert non believers.

Now, young people coming are strongly encouraged to either get married, and do much the same, or go to New York to serve and work for The Watchtower Bible and Tract Society, the organization that publishes Jehovah's Witness literature.

We know no other life and few people outside of the circle. It's a hard and fast rule that we associate with (and marry) only those in the "truth", as they call their teachings. We're not to read publications from other religions, or never set foot in a church.

Not knowing much else about life on the "outside", I view this as normal. I am content for the most part through my teenage years. I believe all of their teachings with all my heart; even on the day my family sits in the car during the funeral of my stepfather's mother because we are not allowed to go into the church.

———

I'm 20 years old, a rebellious but sweet know-it-all as I reach adulthood. It is not very hard for me to accept that my mother, a lifelong researcher, might be leaving the Jehovah's Witnesses. She dares to read other religious literature and compare the Jehovah's Witness bible with other versions, which is forbidden in the years we are members.

Eventually she shares with the family some of the things she found that indicates the "the truth", as the Witnesses refer to the religion, is probably not the only true religion as we have been taught. Actually, I secretly questioned some of the same doctrine but was too lazy to research it thoroughly. I embrace what my mother shows us from the literature she read. Not long after, she and my stepfather leave the religion for good.

Soon, I make my way over to the building which housed our congregation and slip my mandatory letter of intent to disassociate from the Jehovah's Witnesses under the door. Unlike my parents, my motives are not entirely doctrinal. I'm close to the age of twenty-one and getting the sense that there is more to this world beyond the confines of our religion.

I've lived under the relative safety of an organization in which everyone basically plays by the same regimented rules. What if I am missing out on my true, more exciting destiny? It would be nice to discover what my future may hold as I make my mark in the world. I'm too naïve to know that the years of indoctrination will skew my view of the world and of myself for a lifetime.

5 LIFE IN THE REAL WORLD

A few years have and I have adjusted to life outside the confines of the organization in which I grew from a child to young adulthood. I enjoy the new freedoms but still miss some of my Jehovah's Witness friends who can't talk to me anymore since I'm a disassociated 'Witness'.

The strict discipline I developed as a Jehovah's Witness has been beneficial to me on my job. I am always on time and have an excellent work ethic. It is easy for me focus for long periods of time, primarily because we were required to study the bible and other literature for long periods of time. However, I do tend to be more judgmental, mistrustful, and fearful than my colleagues and friends who were never in that religion.

Most of my closest friends these days grew up going to church. Sometimes they laugh good naturedly at my naiveté. My honesty and charm make me a popular and loyal friend. I belong to a tight circle of women in their early twenties. We have fun sharing the drama of our lives as single young ladies in the big city.

I am celebrating my first Christmas this year. I've had fun buying decorations and gifts and saying "Merry Christmas" to everyone I see on the street. This is also the first year that I celebrate my birthday.

I have a steady boyfriend; we are quite serious actually. His name is Eugene. We met in a local music band in which I sing. He is a drummer. We live together unmarried, which is another first which goes against my strict upbringing. I smoke cigarettes now. Once I tried marijuana; it's not my thing. I have decided to stick to social drinking, which is not new to me since I have been doing it since the age of seventeen.

Drinking alcohol was not forbidden in my former religion when I was a member, although drunkenness could lead to being kicked out or, as it is termed, disfellowshipped. Adultery and fornication are also among the sins which could lead to temporary or permanent removal from the religious sect.

I work full time at a bank in the accounts receivable department. It's a good paying job with great medical benefits. I am also in school to learn accounting. I figure the skill could lead me to an even better job in the future.

The truth is I am only fooling myself. I have always disliked math and I am not very good at it. I'll finish this class and then I'm done with this mess.

Lately, every time I take a puff from my cigarette, my lip quivers and I get sick to my stomach. My favorite cologne that Eugene wears also makes me want to vomit when I smell it. It just occurred to me today that I might be pregnant.

My girlfriends advise me to take an in-home pregnancy test that they swear provides accurate results. I've heard about this new test, just never thought I would need it. I will buy one on the way home today and take it before I leave for work early in the morning.

The pregnancy test is positive. Eugene is thrilled. We tell his mother and she is equally happy about the pregnancy. I smile a lot these days as we plan to build a family together.

Telling my parents is another story; I will put it off for as long as possible. I think about the shame and stigmatism that an unplanned, out-of-wedlock pregnancy meant for Jehovah's Witness girls. Here I am, supposed to be the smart one. I'm not supposed to get myself in this situation. But the reality is that I am happy with 'the situation'.

Of course, my sister already knows and she is excited. She has two young daughters; my child will be her first niece or nephew. My closest girlfriends take it in stride and are planning a baby shower.

Tonight we are going to give my parents the news. I ask Eugene to stay in the car so I can tell them alone. I don't know what their reaction will be, especially when they see how positive I am about the pregnancy.

My mother's reaction is less than ecstatic, although I think it is more her reluctance about my choice of boyfriend than the prospect of her third grandchild. My father is grim faced as he asks about my plans. I chat with the two them for a bit and then practically skip to the car to join my boyfriend so we can talk some more about the baby.

This morning I fell to my knees in my first real contraction. When it was over I grabbed my packed bag, grinning from ear to ear, and had Eugene drop me off at

Sherry's house on his way to work. We are in her dining room dancing to Michael Jackson music while she times my contractions and relays the information to my doctor's office.

Many hours later I am gazing at a beautiful tiny baby girl lying on my chest, blinking at me and frowning. Her name is Kimberly. She looks like Eugene and my mother. I can't stop looking at her. It doesn't surprise me that everyone is charmed by our new arrival and I make absolutely no effort to stop the complimentary words and well wishes.

My mother, a nurse, has taken charge of both me and her new granddaughter. The twenty four hour labor is but a memory. The two day stay at the hospital goes by too slowly.

Finally, I am on my way to stay with my mother for a few weeks. I endure taking the obligatory mother-and-baby-in-wheelchair hospital exit picture and we're on our way home.

We get married when the baby is four months old. Eugene wanted to wed sooner but I did not want to go to the altar with a big stomach. As usual, my wishes are granted. Our ceremony is performed at City Hall with his sister, Sherry, and Logan as witnesses. Our daughter grows into an inquisitive toddler who learns everything with the speed of lighting. It is easy to see that as an adult, Kim will have a brilliant mind and superb problem solving abilities.

Five busy years have passed. I have that lip quivering nausea again. This pregnancy is not as unexpected as my first and less scary. Our humble little family is close and fun loving. We have a tight budget like most young families, so for entertainment we mostly visit relatives and have them to our house for gatherings all of the time. My husband and I tough out the lean years of the 1980's; our children are the primary motivation.

I quit my full time job at the bank to open a vintage clothing store with a woman who works with me. She also resigns from her position. She has a disabled daughter and elderly mother she takes care of and my family is dependent upon my income.

Even so, we bravely forge ahead in this venture. We are sure that in time we can make a decent living without the limits of working hours set by an employer. We figure that in time we will be able take time off for family matters as needed without repercussion, something I have always dreamed of achieving. Neither of us has real entrepreneurial experience. I tell Eugene of my plans without asking for his input in the matter. I make the majority of financial choices for the two of us because I am better at handling money.

This solo decision rapidly depletes my meager savings and eats up the little money I receive from selling the tiny stock afforded to employees of the bank. My business partner and I learn too late that prejudice toward minorities and immigrants is alive and well, especially in the wealthy suburb where we open the store. We are among the novice business owners whose businesses go under quickly.

The business has failed after about six months of

repairing broken windows and few customers. I try extra hard to think of ways to save money as it becomes more scarce by the day in our household.

Eugene is providing the sole income in the family. Now the lean years are downright skinny. Feeding and providing for our preschooler and "new baby", as we call the fetus in my belly, are our priorities. It is the city's hottest summer in history and the Detroit Pistons are bringing it home back to back.

This pregnancy, the time between the first contraction and labor is only five hours long. The new baby is tiny, a little over five pounds, a precious baby doll we name Trina. Because she swallowed amniotic fluid during labor, they took her from me the moment she was born to suction her lungs in order to prevent pneumonia.

A couple of hours later, the doctors assure us that she and her lungs are fine. They tell us that four doctors tried and failed to put a suction tube down her throat. She is a fighter; she will carry her feminine strength and intelligence with her into adulthood.

Tears form in our eyes as we gaze down at our sleeping newborn. I can't wait for her big sister to meet her.

———

We have other marital problems besides the shortage of money. Trina's arrival does seem to bind us closer for a period of time. We try to enjoy any good days we have together in an effort to keep our family intact.

Time is passing so quickly. Thankfully, both girls are healthy and thriving. Our finances are in pretty bad shape. We do what we can for our daughters, with very little left over for each other. The girls seem to be fine – unlike our marriage.

6 ON MY OWN

Eleven years have passed since Eugene and I were married. Sadly, even though we still care for one another, we can't seem to overcome the myriad of issues between us. I have moved out of our home to keep me and the girls away from the sometimes volatile discord which exists between me and their father.

I am angry that he is not making the effort to rescue our marriage. And I'm angry at myself for thinking things would work out. I am still young minded and see only my side of the story, which is that Eugene alone is the reason our family is breaking up due to his erratic behaviors and actions. Though those are some of the reasons, we are both still very immature and I share fault as well.

Eugene and I and are both selfish and naïve enough to ignore the real impact that our separation will have on the girls. I am protecting them from a negative environment, but am unable to hide my anger at their father. The bottom line is that we will be the parents of two very special daughters forever. It will be years before I can consider him a friend, though. But it will happen.

———

Now that the divorce is final, I put up a brave front. I adjust to the "single mother" role as any responsible mother should do. I go to work each day to provide for the girls, Eugene sees them off and on. They had no choice in being born or in deciding the breakup of their parents' marriage.

Between child support and my salary, the needs of the children are met. But again, I do not really how much losing the stabilization of the two-parent home is affecting them.

I despise the term "single" parent, mother, or father for the divorced or widowed. It reminds me of the "baby mama" label. I prefer to refer to myself as a "divorced mother".

I reach deep within to remain strong and I pontificate how I was wronged. I hardly ever try to understand his side of the story. I am hurt and disappointed. I think to myself, *He had all the time in the world to get it together. And I gave him the "tools" to do so. We were not his priority; he held himself as the only priority.*

I have a lot to prove. First, I must prove to my daughters that I love them and will take good care of them. They must know that they are safe and what has happened is not their fault.

Many nights I lie awake and pray that am I showing them by example that they can make it in the world despite their circumstances. I question whether I alone can make the girls happy.

I need support, not worry or pity, from my family. They come through for us in all points. Inwardly, I feel insecure and lost, but I never let it show.

With a posture of confidence, I work and take care of

the kids. I also do my fair share of partying with my friends and family and take the girls on outings. When the makeup and heels come off some nights I feel ashamed of my life and lonely most of the time.

Neither my bravado nor the positive attention I get from admirers is enough to make me feel truly happy. All alone one night after the girls are asleep, I face the fact that the only admirer from whom I want attention is my husband. But we are over and done. I accept that the breakup is permanent.

However, I am learning some valuable life lessons as I make a futile attempt to play 'superwoman' during this rough time in my life.

A girlfriend of mine knows the owner of a two-family flat and I move in without a rent deposit. The rent is affordable and the flat is closer to downtown Detroit where I work. There is public transportation nearby to get the girls to school and get myself to work.

But the neighborhood is one of Detroit's poorest and oldest, a far cry from the suburban town home Eugene and I shared. I am concerned about moving there but I know the move will be temporary. I will find better, safer housing after the winter season.

We live there the entire winter without incident. We wait at bus stops and go into stores with people who are not used to the amenities we once had. I am reminded of the genuine kindness and friendliness that are born from the humble human spirit.

The people we encounter can tell we are not from their neighborhood and they sort of look out for us. The bus drivers are courteous and helpful when I have to take my children off the bus at the school and get back on board to head for work.

The experience that winter makes a positive impact on me and serves as a reminder for me to remain humble and reach out to help others in need.

———

I've been single for a few years. I date men but have found no one worthy of being in our lives permanently. A couple of years ago the girls and I moved into a nicer neighborhood in a small home.

The past few months I have had a strong urge to reconnect to Jesus Christ. I accepted Him soon after I left the Witnesses. I feel the call to stop straddling the fence and invite Him back into my life at all cost.

The girls and I attend a little church around the corner from the house we moved into a few months ago. The music, sermons, and fellowship are a comfort to me and some spiritual structure for my daughters.

In the middle of the night a couple of weeks ago I spoke to Him and rededicated my life to His Will yet again. I admitted I am a sinner and that I would accept His forgiveness. As I lay on my back, I asked Him to take my hand and I would hold my two girls in the other as I go forward with my life.

This morning I lie on the floor face down and confess in detail the ugliness and sin of my life to Him. I tell my Savior how I love Him and ask for guidance from above. I cry out my loneliness, fears, anger and guilt. I decide to let go of the negative influences and people that have become my poor substitutes for true companionship during lonely times.

Feeling renewed and refreshed, I go forward feeling content with knowing that though I'm still a sinner, I have connected with God again. The girls and I go to church services but I do not join as a member. During one service Kim accepts Jesus.

Yesterday, one of the gospel television stations that I watch announced that a popular pastor of a large church here is opening his own church in a couple of weeks. My employer, an attorney, gave us a home computer and had it set up for my daughters for the start of this school year. I go online to check for more information about the new church. I find a Christian chat room where people are talking about it and other church news in the area.

Maybe I can find some Christian friends who will be going to the church opening. I log on to the chat room. No one is there. I leave a post asking if anyone from my area will be attending the opening and then go to bed.

The next night I check again and there is one response to my message from a man. His name is William. He lives in the city and writes that he will be attending. He invites me to look at his profile and write back because maybe we can meet there.

The Internet is relatively new, so there are no pictures on our profiles. I read that he is about my age, works for a major car manufacturer, is a long time Christian, has never been married and has no children.

After a few messages back and forth, we agree to meet at the church opening the following Sunday, about a week away. I give him my phone number and we arrange where to meet there. He calls once or twice before Sunday. He sounds friendly, kind, confident, and sincere in his faith.

The moment I see him at the church I just know that he is meant to be in my life for a long time, if not forever. I don't feel a romantic interest, but I immediately want to be his friend. He has a welcoming friendliness and earnestness that draws me in immediately.

Even from our phone calls I sense he is unpretentious, knowledgeable about the word of God, and solid in his faith. He is the type of person who is decent and fair. He was eager and willing to help, with no expectations, when I had questions about the computer or the bible.

He asks, "Would you like to go to lunch after service?"

"Yes."

We talk nonstop for two hours at lunch. He has a hearty appetite. He is the type of person who gives you his full attention as though no one else in the world exists. I enjoy making him laugh; he smiles with his eyes and I can see little crinkles in the corners behind his glasses. Before lunch is done he asks for a date, a real one like dinner and a movie. I say yes.

Months later the two of us are still getting to know one another. We spend time together socializing and visiting different churches. Later, he will tell me he was deliberately trying to take up my time. He is attentive and comforting, a leader. He lets me know that he is looking for a Christian wife. Eventually, he meets my children and family.

I am hesitant to become more involved with him because I view him as a man who is "holier" than me. I smoke cigarettes, drink wine, watch R-rated movies and curse on occasion. I mistakenly perceive that his Christian maturity places him beyond such worldly indulgences.

"I don't want to be a bad influence on you or have you compromise your Christianity," I confess to him one evening.

The crinkles in his eyes, which I love to see, appear in the corners. He quickly dispels my assumption, confirming that Christian doesn't mean perfect or else there would be no need for a Savior.

"Sheila, that's funny because I was going to tell you I smoke cigars. By the way, I do watch R-rated movies. And I enjoy secular music. Some people believe that's a sin."

I laugh and he continues.

"If we were perfect we would not need the blood of

Jesus. It is our job to strive to please Him because of the meaning of His sacrifice." He shares scriptures to back up his words.

Reading and discussing the bible become an enjoyable activity, along with dining out, movies, and other entertainment. He wins over the girls because he treats both them and me very well. My mother, always skeptical, sees him as the Lord's gift to me. I'm beginning to agree.

One winter evening we pull in the parking lot at the movie theater. We are in good spirits, chatting and laughing along the ride. I jump out of the passenger seat before he gets out of the car and pull snow from the roof of the car. I chuck a snowball over the roof and into his head when he gets out. He laughs, his chuckle big and hearty as usual.

He comes around the car and takes my hand and we walk toward the theater, talking as we walk. Without looking at me or missing a beat, he tosses a snowball in my face. I never see it coming. I crack up laughing. And fall in love.

———

Three months later:

"I don't know whether I should marry again. I have my daughters to think of."

"One day your girls are going to grow up and have lives of their own. You should have someone to take care of you, too."

"Yeah, maybe."

Two weeks later:

"Please let me treat you like you deserve to be treated. I promise I will show your girls what to look for in a man when they are old enough to have husbands. Will you marry me?"

"Yes."

———

It's the night of Valentines Day. He places the beautiful ring on my finger and offers promises with a kiss. We'll be married this June.

7 AGAIN, HAPPINESS

Each passing day, we get to know each other more. He sees what it's like to be in the constant company of three females. For all the good and the bad, for the better or the worse - nothing is a deal breaker for either of us.

He consistently demonstrates his love and devotion for me and my children. He is attentive, patient and kind; his priority is to incorporate the word of God into our lives. I get a chance to again flex my wifely muscles and take care of him and our home the best I can.

His mother, Elaine, confirms her son's desire to be a good husband. She tells me that he dated women but refused to settle for less than someone he was sure he could build a quality life with.

One day Elaine tells me that her son made a vow that he would not be like his deceased father, who proved to be unfaithful and abusive to her for years before his death from a heart attack. Like a man on a mission, William's actions show that he intends to keep his vow.

As the day of the wedding day grows closer it is obvious that Kim, now a teenager, is not exactly thrilled at the prospect of gaining a stepfather. She is, of course, polite when in William's presence. She graciously accepts the gifts and other ways in which he tries to win her over. She talks with him and shows respect but to me she's not too enthusiastic about our engagement.

I realize that I did not ask specifically for my children's "blessings" on the upcoming marriage. I did not doubt that the man I was going to marry was God's gift to us. I've said to him, as well as friends and family, that I was unable to choose the best man for my life – so I let the Lord do it this time.

Besides, I was raised to believe that minor children follow what their parents choose in life until their old enough to make their own decisions for their lives.

The wedding day is getting closer. I sense that it is necessary to address the reason for Kim's feelings. We talk about her love for her biological father and her fear I will be hurt again. Trina, as a small girl, appears to be happy and adores my fiancé and the perks she and her sister receive.

Nothing or no one will ever come between my love for my daughters. I know that Kim, as the oldest, is a little hesitant about the new family dynamic. We talk about how William will be the support we need with some of the burdens we have been facing alone the last four years. I assure my daughter that I love her and she could never be replaced.

It makes no sense to force the girls to "feel" any particular way about William or our marriage. William is wise enough not to try and be "daddy", but to let the relationship with the girls fall into place naturally. In time, Kim will grow to trust my decision.

What I don't know is that ten years from now, she will be getting married. My phone will ring...

"Mama, it's me. I've decided to ask William to walk me down the aisle and to do the father-daughter dance," Kim will say when I answer.

"What about your father?"

"He will definitely be there. And I will dance with him too."

I'll have tears in my eyes as I watch them walk the aisle together as father and daughter on a hot day in August, two years before he dies.

————

The weather is pleasantly warm this evening in June. The air is humid because it has been raining for a couple of days. My mother, father, daughters, fiancé and I meet at the large union hall just outside of the city. The nuptials will take place here in the room we will decorate to look like a small wedding chapel. The reception will be in the adjacent banquet room

Jazz, soul and R&B music are playing loudly as William sets up the stereo system. The rest of us are busy putting up decorations and setting up tables and chairs.

My father is walking around looking over the facility. He is not a talkative or affectionate man by nature. He is known for offering sound advice to our family since he married my mother when I was a child. Tonight he is friendly but his facial expression is unreadable. Since he has several health problems, I assume he may not be feeling well and is toughing it out as usual.

Ours will not be a traditional wedding. Although we both are Christians, we have not joined with a particular denomination or church yet. We decide to have our wedding and reception here and have his Christian minister friend to officiate.

The ceremony will begin with the start of Kenny G's song, *The Moment*. Trina will walk down the aisle first, followed by her sister. After a brief pause I will walk, unescorted, to meet William at the altar, which is a wedding arch covered in white and cream silk flowers. William's best friend and the minister will be standing with him there.

Everyone seems pleased with the decorations; the hall is elegant and festive. I'm excited, not nervous at all. William makes no effort to hide his eagerness. Since the night he proposed he has been saying that he will be "glad when we get to the other side of this thing" (meaning the wedding). That is an expression he uses whenever he is faced with a serious problem, looking forward to something special, or making an important decision.

Two hours have passed and we are getting ready to leave the venue. We talk about tomorrow while we pack up materials and tools. My father interrupts our conversation.

"We should walk through the ceremony. Just in case," he says.

"What are you thinking?" I ask him.

I still cannot read the expression on his face.

"Well, we can't be too sure. Let's make sure it goes smoothly," is his answer.

We agree that his idea is a good one and take our places as we discussed. My daughters and I go to the restroom area where we will walk down a short hallway and then into the ceremony room. William stands at the front of the room with a Cheshire cat grin on his face. My mother is set to start the music on his cue.

I hear the song begin and send out the girls one by one. In the short seconds before I am to follow, love and gratefulness flow over my body like lava from a volcano. When I enter the chapel room, I see my father standing on the outside aisle, halfway to the altar. He is openly weeping.

We are finished with the run-through and it looks as though things should go smoothly tomorrow.

My father hugs me tightly and says, "I am so happy for you. He is a good man."

The next morning I wake up to mild chaos. Relatives from out of town arrive. Including my daughters, there are five other ladies dressing themselves in the two small bathrooms of my home.

I am dressing at home because the banquet hall does not have facilities for grooming or dressing. I can't seem to get my hairpiece exactly right and no one has volunteered to assist me. I'm annoyed. I suck it up with one last look in the mirror and the head downstairs.

My brother-in-law escorts me to the car and drives us to the hall. We arrive with plenty of time to spare. The weather is still warm with intermittent showers. The ground is damp and muddy so I am careful not to dirty my shoes walking to the building.

The door that leads to the room where the ceremony will take place is slightly open. As I walk by on my way to the restroom I get a glimpse inside and see that several guests have arrived early and taken their seats.

It seems as though only a few seconds have passed and then I hear the first beautiful notes of *The Moment*. Happy butterflies take flight in my stomach and my hands shake slightly. Trina, then Kim, goes before me. Both girls are wearing white dresses; to me they look like angels.

As I walk down the aisle my eyes meet William's and he nods slightly. I know that he is confirming he is feeling what he has told me many times over the last six months, which is that he is "the envy of all men". I smile and am blinded briefly from the flash of the photographer's camera.

Within a matter of minutes I am a wife…again. We walk hand-in-hand into the reception room with hearts full of hope.

8 JOURNEY TO GEORGIA

After two years, the four of us are accustomed to being under the same roof. We live with the same mixture of disagreements, misunderstandings, bonding, commitment, and love as most families. William and I have no doubt that the marriage was destined to last a lifetime. Both daughters have settled in to the new family arrangement.

We weather the storms of life together, like the death of his mother, health concerns, and finances. I have to admit that, even though I just turned forty, I do not have the energy I once had. Working full time and keeping the family and home in order takes so much more effort for me recently. Most evenings I come home from work and only have energy enough to get ready for bed.

I have been working about five years as a paralegal in an immigration law office. I have climbed the ranks and have my own secretary, office overlooking the Detroit River, and nice salary plus benefits. I enjoy my job and get along well with the entire staff. One evening when I come home exhausted, William brings up the subject of me staying home full time.

"I want to be sure you know that all I want to do is take care of you and the girls."

I think, *where did that come from?*

"I appreciate that so much. You are a great provider.

I am ok. But I'm used to working. Plus I don't feel everything should be on you."

By now I recognize the look on his face. This subject has been on his mind for a while. He wants to talk about it.

"I agree the two incomes have been helpful. We are able to travel more and buy some of the things we want.

But how long can you keep going like this without sacrificing your health or time with me and the girls? I think we should pray about it."

My mind, but not my mouth, says, *Pray about what?*

William lays out his case. Right now, we can be comfortable financially with his income alone. I can't deny that I am tired or that my career has taken a back seat to my family obligations. I'm not as focused on work now.

More than anything he wants to be the protector and provider as mandated in the bible. Still, it's a big decision. I do agree to pray for guidance.

———

I have been praying about it. I ask God, "Do you really want me to quit this great job that You gave me?"

God is not answering, at least not the answer I want to hear. I come up with a compromise. I will work part time at the office and bring work home to finish in the evening.

I tell William. His response is a slight smile and a hug. I'm feeling confused and a little aggravated at his lack of enthusiasm about my plan. He tells me that whatever I decide is fine with him. I think it is good plan.

Over time I learn that what I see as smugness is actually a peaceful serenity he gets when he's praying about a matter and has given it over to God.

One month later, I am more exhausted than ever, sometimes to the point of tears. We sit down for another talk about the work situation.

"I watch you working, keeping this house, getting the girls back and forth to school. You are truly a Proverbs 31 wife, you know that"?

Flatterer.

"Sheila I fully understand that you are not the type of woman to just sit around all day. But to be honest, I don't like the idea that you have to punch somebody's time clock."

"What do you mean, that you never wanted me to work?" I ask.

"I would never say I don't want you to work because your business skills and talents are part of what make me love you. But I never intended for my wife to have to kill herself to keep food on the table that I am supposed to provide."

I chastise myself for coming off as ungrateful. How many women would give anything to have such a blessing?

I tell him that truthfully I could use a break but that I won't hesitate to go back to work if we need the money. But I do know my husband; there's more to this than he's saying.

We have a long discussion; he wants to make sure that I can be content working from home. Unhappy wife, unhappy life, and all those types of subjects are discussed.

"I'm really starting to get the hang of the Internet, William. Maybe I can work from home on the computer to make money."

"I will fund and support any type of work you want to do from home. It's worth it to me to have more time with you," he says with a wink.

I get it. But I'm not a bit upset about it. I could use a little more time alone myself. We both laugh.

I give my job notice that I'm leaving. I'm relieved. For a short time I supplement the household income doing some of the legal paperwork from the law office from home. Then I start a small business building and developing websites for community organizations. Together, William and I also develop affiliate retail websites which brings in extra money.

Far from perfect, my life overall provides me with the spiritual, mental, and physical contentment I sought for many years. I make the work from home transition and find balance.

———

William first mentioned moving to Georgia just before Kim graduated from high school.

"You know, I've always liked Georgia. The people are friendlier there."

"Oh, yeah? I haven't been down south since I was a child," I reply.

"I used to go to Macon every year. I remember how everyone said good morning when I boarded the bus each day."

I look at him with one eyebrow raised. I sense this is more than small talk. Maybe he just wants to visit his mother's relatives one day.

"That's nice. I heard they are friendlier and that educational standards are higher there," I say.

Every now and then William mentions moving to Georgia. When he does, the look on my face says I'm not buying what he's trying to sell. Sometimes I think I see that "smug/not smug" smile on his face.

One birthday he takes me to Atlantic City. On the snowy drive home through the mountains, he mentions again that he would like to move to Georgia when he retires. I am angry; an emotion I often use to mask fear.

"Are you serious about this?"

"Yes, Sheila. I am serious. I have been telling you this

for a couple of years now."

"Why do you want to move somewhere where we don't know anybody?"

"I want to retire somewhere I will feel at peace. And where I don't have to shovel my way out of the house every winter. It will be harder to be in this climate when we're older."

Was that a wisecrack about my age? I let it go, but I feel the fear inside of me increase. My heart is beating fast.

"You didn't find me in the back woods of Georgia and that's not where you are going to take me. Away from my family. Somewhere I don't know anybody..."

I fold my arms across my chest. For good measure, I don't say another word to him all the way back down the mountain. Unfazed, he continues to drive carefully along the hazardous roads. I know I see that small upturn in his lips out of the corner of my eye. Soon enough, we are talking as usual.

Something tells me I won't get my way on this.

I have been praying about moving to Georgia the past few months. I'm not as adamant about not relocating as before, but I'm still not entirely convinced.

He hasn't said as much about moving to Georgia lately. I know it isn't because he's changed his mind. William is a proud man; it isn't in his nature to pressure or badger me or anyone else for anything. Maybe that's why he's been silent on the matter. His way is to take matters to prayer and then go on living life to the fullest until he gets an answer. I admire that, because I worry and pray at the same time.

I wake up very early one morning and hear two words in my heart: Why not? Immediately, I know there is no real reason not to follow my husband to Georgia. It will not be easy to move away, but I trust William. I love him and want him to spend his retirement years where he will be happiest, especially after all he's done for us. I feel calm and assured.

When he calls me on his lunch hour I ask, "When are we moving to Georgia?"

Later, when I ask was he surprised I had given in, he said he was not. He told me that he had asked God to change not just my mind, but my heart. Then he would know that I gave in to God's will, not to him.

We fly to Georgia several times before the move to look for a house. We are charmed by the state's lush greenery and abundance of sun and flowers. The realtor finds us a nice home in one of the best school districts for Trina to attend her senior year of high school.

Within two weeks of his retirement, William, Trina, and I head to Georgia after selling our home in Detroit. Kim decides not to move. She's a responsible twenty two year old, but saying goodbye is agonizing to say the least. It will be seven years of back and forth visits before Kim moves to Georgia. My mother and father also decline our offer to bring them South.

I am concerned for Trina. She sorely misses her sister, friends, and the familiarity of home. The three of us spend our days exploring the state, eating out, decorating the house, and other simple activities. My youngest makes a valiant effort not to show us her unhappiness.

I think it is a good idea to find a little church where we could meet some people as well as worship. We join a tiny fellowship of believers who welcome us in right away. Being such a small church our help is needed for every task, from leading praise and worship to cleaning the building. We remain members for about a year and a half.

By this time William and I are comfortable with living in the South. We venture all over to museums, historical landmarks, and other attractions. Trina has left the nest to bravely find her own way. We spend more time alone doing the things we love so much.

Another year passes and William discovers a much larger church and we go to two services. He agrees with the doctrine and likes the pastor's teaching. We attend for some time and then join the church. Once again, we are kept busy with many activities, praise, worship, and we serve on various ministry committees.

We make lots of church friends, which is my definition of people we are very close to but do not socialize with outside of church activities. There are one or two ladies whom I've become friends with and see outside of church now and then.

Trina shows no interest in attending or getting involved with this church. Since her high school graduation, she spends most of her time working, hanging out with her friends, and attending school part time.

William's knowledge and love of the deeper things in the bible make him a wonderful teacher of sound doctrine. My spiritual gifts lean toward hospitality, inspiration, and giving. Eager to serve, we sign up for a one year ministry course and graduate together.

At the graduation ceremony William seems to be in a bad mood, which is unlike his pleasant personality. He kinds of fusses around with what he's going to wear and is sort of quiet on the ride to church.

The graduates are seated on one side of the church. We are talking, laughing, and taking pictures. My husband is still somewhat quiet. I think maybe he's coming down with a cold or something. The ceremony ends and we stand at the front of the church to get our certificates and pictures, go to lunch, then head home.

Three weeks later I know what I was afraid to see on the Sunday of our graduation. My husband was not in a bad mood. He was not catching a cold. He was dying.

After his funeral, my sister and I look at the pictures from the day of the graduation.

"My brother didn't look like he felt so good," she says as she looks at a picture of him.

"I think he hadn't been feeling good for a while and didn't want to tell me."

William took pride in being a manly-man. And he

went out of his way to not worry me about anything. I wonder if that's why he didn't tell me. These thoughts tear my heart to pieces. Perhaps I am wrong, my musings could just be my sad state of mind. I am comforted that he attended and completed ministry school. He was so proud of that accomplishment; I have a copy of his graduation certificate placed in his closed casket.

I play and replay the days preceding his death, obsessed with the thought that there was a sign I missed. I do know that William didn't want to move us to Georgia so he could come here to die. He wanted to live. He was full of life, love and laughter. I'm glad he had the chance to live where he was happy for his last five years on earth.

9 CALL IN THE PROFESSIONALS

October 28, 2011

I am like a robot as I drive this morning. No emotion shows on my face. My movements are stiff and minimal. Today is my first visit ever with a psychotherapist. Last month, my medical doctor observed that I showed symptoms of PTSD and strongly suggested I seek behavioral health help, so I made this appointment.

I've been thinking and acting strangely the past few months since William's funeral, far beyond grieving my loss. I'm scaring myself and maybe even the people who love me.

I am resistant because it is foreign to me to share anything personal with someone I don't know. My people are not the kind to get involved with psychotherapy of any kind.

But I think I'm losing control of my mind. It would be tragic if I go completely insane; me, the so called smart one. I choose to numb myself to get through whatever lies ahead this morning. But something has to give; I'm going to get professional help in addition to the spiritual assistance and family support I receive.

I don't turn on the radio as I usually do when I drive. Normally, my mind goes into overdrive when silence surrounds me. I think about things I have to do, I pray, go over family or other issues—my brain in a state of categorized chaos. Only now I don't hear a thing as I pull into the parking lot in dead silence. Except that humming down inside me that never stops; it only changes volume. Right now it's on medium low volume.

The parking lot is still pretty much empty since my appointment at the medical center is one of the first of the day. I don't get lost and have no trouble finding the building in Alpharetta, Georgia. But I don't celebrate this small victory today. I have been here a lot over the past few years.

The building is the hub for the offices of medical specialists and internists, including the offices of one of William's husband's specialty doctors he came to regularly. It is also where I brought him to see a medical doctor on the last day he left home alive.

I sit in the car and recall that day…

My robust husband is weak for the third day in a row with flu symptoms. He has a rash on his head and chest. He holds his head off the pillow slightly.

"If I don't feel better by tomorrow, I'll go to the doctor."

"Ok. Get some rest."

It is the first Monday morning in June. I stand in the doorway of our bedroom and watch him try to sit up in bed to talk. By now his eyes have gone from pink to a deep red hue. The rash has spread to his torso and he still has a fever. A part of me wants to believe he has the flu, or even measles.

I go downstairs and boot up the computer to do some editing work. The humongous room is his "man cave", complete with full sized pool table and over sized television. One corner of this room serves as my office. The room is on the shady side of the house and is always cool. This morning it is cold.

I sit at the computer and begin working on a project for a client. I'm having trouble concentrating. After about ten minutes I stop working. The house is quiet. I am shaking. Maybe it's the temperature in this room. A nervous nagging starts in my stomach.

I think about my father, who is ill in Michigan. My sister and I have been talking recently about how he keeps avoiding going to the doctor. I get up from the computer and go to the kitchen. I call William's doctor's office and speak with the nurse, who knows the both of us.

"I think William has the measles and I don't want to catch them."

I chuckle, trying to keep my voice light. I let go a slight sigh of relief when the nurse takes the same tone.

"What's going on with him?" she asks. I hear her smile.

"He's had a fever since Saturday. And a rash that started on his head but has spread. He's not eating at all. He's also lethargic."

"Describe the rash."

"It's like hundreds of tiny raised bumps," I tell her.

"Has he had the measles before?"

"He says he had them as a child." Again, I try to laugh but the humor gets stuck in my throat.

My husband told me that he had measles as a child when I asked yesterday. But looking at the rash I doubted him, thinking maybe he was mistaken. The nurse asks me to hold the line. She comes back on the line in about two minutes.

"The doctor wants you to bring him in, let me give you a time."

I detect a change in her tone. I suppose that, because he has other medical conditions, they want to err on the side of caution.

Then she pauses. "Oh wait, his doctor does not have any open appointments today. Take him to the medical center in Alpharetta where his specialty doctor has an office. See the medical doctor there."

My hand shakes slightly as I write down the name of the doctor. William has an appointment with his own doctor next week. I wonder why he couldn't just come in then. But I don't ask. I thank her and go upstairs to our bedroom.

William is asleep with his back to me. I touch him lightly to wake him. The sheet covering his body is very warm.

"The doctor wants you to come in today, not tomorrow," I say softly.

"They have made an appointment for you at the medical center because your doctor is booked today."

He looks worse to me; I can't quite put my finger on in what way. To my surprise, he does not put up a fight. Slowly, he begins to get out of bed to get dressed.

I go downstairs to make sure food and water are left for the cat. I wait for him in the man cave; the driveway is just outside of its sliding glass doors. The huge hardwoods on both sides of the house make the room dark, despite its four tall windows.

As I sit on his man-sofa I see my reflection in the huge television screen it faces. *I don't look so hot myself actually,* I think. My face is pale and my lips are turned down. I am breathing fast and shallow. I hear him making his way down the stairs. I sit up straight and put a smile on my face.

He's dressed in his beloved Georgia Bulldogs jersey, a pair of blue jean walking shorts and sandals. He is moving very slowly. And complaining — something this patient, even tempered man never does. Outside, he attempts to open the driver's door of the car.

"Oh, no you don't. You're sick so I'm driving." Again, he doesn't protest. He enjoys driving and I normally like being a passenger. The atmosphere itself feels odd in this moment in time.

I slide behind the wheel. He makes his way to the passenger side and gets in the car. The sun shines brightly; the sky is a vibrant baby blue. I smell pine, magnolias, and the leather of the car seats. I hear birds chirping. It's a beautiful early summer morning.

"It's so cold. I'm so cold," he moans during the ride to the doctor.

I turn off the air conditioning and leave the windows raised. I am very warm but he is so cold that he's shaking.

In this brilliant daylight I can see that the whites of his eyes are now a solid dark red. There's something strange about his skin, too. I can also see there are so many bumps now that they seem to be coming together forming (*What am I seeing?*) something like blisters. My mind, on its own, decides that I will not process how he looks or it will frighten me. I need to be brave for my husband.

He lays his head back on the headrest. I tell him I know he doesn't feel well, and that he will get better. I pray aloud for him, and for us. He's awake but his eyes are closed. He keeps repeating he is cold.

I'm sweating as I drive, glancing over at William now and then. My heart is heavy and real worry is gradually creeping its way into my mind and heart. We finally pull into the medical center parking lot. He is too weak and cannot walk. I leave him in the car and run inside and get a wheelchair to take him into the building...

Today, four months later, I circle the same parking lot to find a space far in the back where it will be unlikely that people will be around when I return. I try to avoid looking at the space where I parked the day I brought William here. I stop the car. Then I stare, as though in a trance, at where we were parked that morning, and continue to relive the moment in clear detail…

I see myself running inside the building, coming back and struggling to get him in the wheelchair. I see the red Georgia Bulldog sandals on the silver metal footrests of the wheelchair. I feel the sweat on the back of my neck. I hear myself telling my sister on the phone that I have him at the doctor's office and will have to call her back later. *Stop now or you will remember some things that will break your heart.* I shake my head quickly.

A few minutes later I force myself to keep driving and make sure I find a parking space at the far end of the lot. I walk into the medical center and make my way to the third floor, to the office marked Behavioral Health. It's as though I'm outside of myself, like I'm not really here.

I never thought I would be walking through the door of a psychiatrist's office. My hand hesitates to open it as pride and fear take over my brain for a moment. My next thought is that if I don't do this I won't have a chance of returning to normal. This thought motivates me to bear down and endure whatever this decision will bring.

I've been drowning in madness and I'm scared for my sanity. My pretense is over; I no longer have doubt that there is something serious going on with me. I pull the door handle and step inside.

As I wait for the doctor my heart is pounding, I am dizzy and nauseated, something that happens regularly when I am not at home. I'm fighting not to leave and go back to my house where it is safe.

Briefly, I ponder if I am shaming my family, church, or my husband's memory by seeking mental health assistance. Does this mean I reject the healing of God? I can't figure it out right now. I want to survive. For months I have known I need extra help. My skin is crawling. My inner hum is louder, maybe even escaping my lips.

I need help however I can get it, and fast. From God, the doctors, people who love and care about me. Please, all hands on deck before I am lost forever in this madness.

I know nothing about the woman I am seeing except her name, Brianna Olen. I requested a female therapist. As I wait I try to formulate a plan for how I will handle a situation I've never faced. Will I tell her details like how I tap my fingernails all day or otherwise risk being extremely uncomfortable and off kilter? Does she have to know I make sure I tap the walls as I walk around the house, how I tap tables and arms of the furniture to soothe myself?

I recall the day Kim made me aware of the tapping. I was sitting in the back seat of her car on one of her visits from Michigan.

"What's that noise, Mom?"

I'm embarrassed as hell as I realize I am tapping on the plastic part of the car door with my fingernails.

"Sorry." I tap lightly on the seat cushion for the rest of the ride.

As seconds turn to minutes I take a guess at the impact therapy will have on my life. If I tell her that I want to die, will she have me committed or make me take psychotropic medicine? There are too many things going on with me. Surely she won't have time to listen to all of them today.

I constantly check the doors and windows, day and night; I am exhausted from lack of sleep. I keep going back and reading my dead husband's death certificate and obituary. Ok, maybe she'll tell me that part is normal for a widow.

I also spend hours upon hours reading and re-reading the medical records of the last two weeks of his life. I go on the Internet and look up the words in the report that I don't understand. I constantly study about the condition which took his life.

There is too much that goes on for me to name. I am not even close to who I used to be. Perhaps all of the things I do are caused by my grief.

One particular incident alarmed me to the point of making this appointment. A couple of weeks ago I'm in the car sitting at a red light, waiting to make a left turn when the arrow turns green. Oncoming traffic is flowing toward me on the opposite side of the road. I tap, tap, and tap on the center console. I hear a voice counting inside my head; it is my voice.

I am counting the seconds until I think the green garbage truck on the other side will cross the intersection, based upon its speed, so I can turn my car into its path. Hands on the steering wheel, I get to "7, 8" and something snaps. I scream out loud, "No....! Wait!" The faces of my daughters come to my mind. I wait for traffic to clear and make the turn safely when it does.

I make it home and slam my keys on the counter. I pace the house, trapped between anger for not making the turn and guilt that I intended to so. A couple of hours pass before I come out of my state and see that I have been crawling around in tears and vomit.

Yes, I think I will tell her about that one incident. Maybe getting it out will stop that one from happening again. Yuck.

———

My thoughts are interrupted when I hear my named called. Dr. Olen is holding the door to the offices open. She has a bright smile that I can't return.

I am grateful that she's friendly but her stare makes me uncomfortable, smile or not. I'm sure I will not make a real connection with her; she is at least twelve years younger than I. She's being very gracious, though, so I sit down and look her in the eye.

Her voice is soft. She takes a seat across the room.

"Tell me why you are here."

"I...really don't know," are all the words I can say

before I burst into a fit of anguish.

It's almost an hour later and I am about to leave this small room. Most of the hour, I see her as though she is far away. She's no longer smiling but her eyes are kind.

I hear myself speaking about the manner in which my husband died, but tell her nothing beyond the date of his death. My breathing is so fast I am panting. She tells me to take deep breaths; I am unable to do so.

My eyes are almost swollen shut and my nose is stuffy. I feel dead but I'm angry because I'm not. Mostly, I want my husband here with me and I tell her so.

I can't meet the eyes of this stranger whom I let see me in such a state. I look down at my hands that hold damp, shredded tissue. I am rocking back and forth. I won't tell her today about so many of the things that have been happening to me, including the incident with the car, because I'm too wasted. And I'm afraid of what she will say.

Once I am somewhat calm, she asks me several general questions concerning my memories of what happened with William, my sleep patterns, my actions. I answer them honestly, my head still down.

"I believe you have Post Traumatic Stress Syndrome."

Then she reads from a printout about the condition, which she hands to me. My eyes are blurry but I feel relief that there is a name for what I'm experiencing and possible treatment. I can't speak, but I trust her.

I let her make another appointment for the following week.

10 DIAGNOSIS

Today is the second of many therapy sessions that I will attend in the years that lay ahead. I am in a dark mood as I enter the quiet, dimly lit office with no windows. Although the office is large, Dr. Olen sits six feet away facing me so the setting is intimate, but she is not sitting so close that it makes me feel uncomfortable.

My chair is against a wall next to a low table that holds tissues, a plant, and a clock that faces the therapist. I am having trouble slowing down my breathing. I cannot control my fingers from tapping on the metal arms of the chair in which I sit.

She smiles broadly as we settle in. "How are you, Sheila?"

I blink rapidly in a futile attempt to hold back tears. "Um…not too good."

"Take some deep, slow breaths." she says.

I watch as she demonstrates how to slow my breathing. My eyes are closed and my brow is wrinkled. By this time my nose is stopped; any breathing is difficult, slowly or otherwise. My eyes drop quickly to my lap each time I make eye contact with the therapist.

"What are you feeling right now?" I hear her question over the tapping noise my nails are making on the chair.

I reach to my left for a tissue. I wonder how much

longer the session will last. I dab at my wet face.

"Hurt and pain. That's all I feel."

She encourages me to continue to express what I am feeling. That is not at all easy for me. As in our first session, sadness engulfs me like a tidal wave each time I try to speak. She listens patiently for a few minutes, watching me intently. But I don't sense she is judging me. In fact, she encourages me to let the tears flow.

I notice her glance at my hands and I attempt to stop the tapping. Her voice is soft but she speaks clearly. She tells me she is sorry for my loss and asks a series of questions about what I have been experiencing since my husband died. I sense she is sincere, patient, and competent, so I try to open up a little more.

I tell her how much I miss my husband and of my suicidal thoughts. This time I do mention the incident when I considered turning the car into oncoming traffic. Initially, I respond to her queries with a word or two. I feel exposed; like the roof of my home has been snatched off while I'm bathing.

She gently probes so that I will open up to her about what I experience on a daily basis. I feel raw and vulnerable. I reveal to her that I constantly check doors and windows in my home. She listens attentively as I explain my consuming fear.

Her next set of questions address how I feel physically. I'm tired from lack of sleep. She asks what keeps me awake. I tell her how on the nights I do doze off

I am suddenly awakened. Though I try, I can't identify what awakes me, though it happens at least four times a week.

"I don't know," I say. "All I know is that I doze off and then I am yanked awake."

"What do you feel when you wake up?" she asks.

"I feel very frightened. And I feel like I'm going to die."

"What do you feel physically?"

"My heart races, I feel dizzy, and I shake. Then I cry because I can't go back to sleep. I take Benadryl sometimes to help me sleep."

She turns to her computer and then back to me. Then asks more questions about what I feel or think on a regular basis follow. I share with her that I almost jump out of my skin when I hear sudden, loud noises. Dr. Olen periodically looks at the computer screen.

She tells me that I have all the symptoms of Post Traumatic Stress Syndrome. Her diagnosis is based on what I have told her and the information she has been referring to about the condition. She goes over a checklist of symptoms with me that affirm her assessment.

I raise my red, swollen eyes to meet those of the stranger speaking to me. I am feeling a combination of relief and misery. Recently, it had crossed my mind that I may have PTSD but I dismissed them. I thought only people who had been in military combat or victims of assault could have PTSD. I tell her this.

She explains that severe trauma of any kind can result in PTSD symptoms.

"I encourage you to learn more about the condition. It will help you to understand what is happening with you and to and figure out a plan that will help you."

We finish up the session and confirm our appointment next week. I don't have all of the answers to what is happening. But I do sense that what she has told me is most likely the truth. Now that I have a diagnosis, I can most likely be cured in a few sessions and move on with my life being a normal grieving widow without the extras I have been experiencing.

When I leave her office with a printed summary of my visit, my eyes fixate on the words next to "Diagnosis of This Visit": Post Traumatic Stress Disorder and Major Depression, Recurrent. Halfway to my house I pull the car over. I can't drive; I feel overwhelmed.

Twenty minutes later I make my way back home. I am lonesome, lost, and as it happens, alone for the day. Which is probably for the best. A bit of hope pops up now and then. This all will be over soon, by whatever means it takes. And then I can mourn William's death like any other typical widow. And be Sheila again.

11 MILESTONE OR MISTAKE?

Recently, I made the choice to fight for my life. To spend the rest of my days straddling the fence is not an option. I either commit to living or commit to dying.

I chose to live with as much quality and dignity as possible. I know it will be a hard road, but I am eager for my life to take on some resemblance of a so called normal existence. Perhaps in my enthusiasm, I jumped head first into the fight long before I was properly trained and equipped. I hit brick walls when I push myself too much.

Thanksgiving is tomorrow. It is the start of the first winter holiday season since William's death. We always loved the winter holidays so I'm not surprised that I'm enjoying preparing food for tomorrow's feast.

The meal will be pretty much the same delicious Thanksgiving menu the women in my family have cooked since I was a teenager, though each of us has added a few dishes of our own over the years. I believe I am just fine, almost at the end of this nightmarish mental seesaw. The clock reads 7:30 p.m.

Michael and Kim will be here from Michigan any minute. I have cooked extra food for them because I know they'll be hungry after the twelve hour drive. Some of my favorite music is playing in the background as I work. The scent of holiday food fills the air and the house looks festive. Just like it does every year.

About ten years ago I started putting Christmas decorations up by the day after Thanksgiving, at the latest. With the exception of the dining room, which is set for Thanksgiving dinner, the house is a Christmas holiday delight.

Everything but the turkey and a couple other dishes are done by Wednesday night. That way, I am more relaxed by the time we sit down to eat and I can enjoy the holiday with everyone.

It was not easy to sort through all of the lovely holiday mementos we collected over the years. The memories of the many Christmases we enjoyed so much are bittersweet, for lack of a better word. But I have not been in the mood (or too afraid of the crowds) to shop for new decorations. So I come up with an idea.

I revamp the decorations. I create and rearrange vignettes, themes, and color schemes using what I had in the attic. I carefully avoid the boxes near the back of the attic which hold William's collection of Christmas villages he loved to set up each year. There is an abundance of other decorations to work with.

I stand in the living room and look around. Yes, this looks like Christmas – a fresh start Christmas. I'm pleased. Everyone else will be happy and proud of me for getting through such a dreadful crisis so quickly. I'm so glad it's over. I think I'm healed with just a few tweaks to go.

I'm setting the table with the Thanksgiving decorations when Kim and Michael arrive. Trina's been here for a couple of hours. As always, we are thrilled to see each other. Both of my daughters and son-in-law keep me company as I finish up for the evening.

Sherry and her family will be joining us for dessert and drinks tomorrow evening. I feel the overall anxiety and panic that the therapist talked to me about last month, but nothing alarming. The happiness I feel about being with my loved ones for the holiday is all the therapy I need.

A couple of hours later I go to bed content that the ones I love are sleeping under the same roof with me. I'm grateful that my bedroom and bathroom are separated from everyone in case I have a difficult night. I check the doors and windows only once.

It's Thanksgiving night and dinner is over; the holiday spirit is in full swing. There are about twelve family members here who live here in Atlanta. We are having a real good time.

I deliberately ignore the feeling that I'm floating away and watching the scene from the ceiling. *Oh no you don't. Not the crazies. Not tonight.*

We make it a point not to talk about William, it's hard since we all know he loved the holidays. I mention his name and I see it makes us all uncomfortable and so I change the subject. The party goes well into the night.

At one point my niece, who is playing DJ, unknowingly puts on a song that immediately made me feel upset and I start to cry. It was a favorite of William's. No one knew that I sang it to him in the hospital a few days before he died.

Kim caught my reaction and asked her to take it off, which she did. The party continued without another hitch. I even went with my other niece to the mall at 2:00 a.m. so she could take advantage of a Black Friday sale.

Soon after, the festivities end and my sister and her family go home. We straighten up the house and everyone retires for the night. I hide that something is not right with me.

Even tonight, after a joyous occasion, I battle the feeling that I so badly want to die. It dumps itself all over me as soon as I close my bedroom door. Then I feel guilty for thinking about it when so many people love and depend on me, plus they are hurting too.

Did I pressure myself to celebrate the holiday to prove that things were back to normal? The pressure did not come from my family, because they only want what's best for me. I have to face that I am probably to blame for what I'm feeling., that I am my own saboteur.

Nonetheless, next month I will celebrate Christmas like I have every year-for much the same reason. It's all part of the fight to get right, I suppose.

I loathe having a condition which takes control of my mind and emotions at will. Me - the problem solving, nurturing, strategizing rock. Who am I now? This is a mess. I go to bed, kind of sleep and like most mornings I am disappointed, to say the least, when I wake.

12 CAN'T SAY GOODBYE

January 25, 2012

It's 2:30 am. The house is dark with the exception of the television I leave on at night on low volume to help chase away the night terrors. My phone rings. It's Sherry.

"Hey, Mama just got the call that he's taken a turn for the worse and she should get to the hospital."

"Is he gone?" I ask her.

"No not yet. But we know what that call means. I'll call you back when I find out more."

I got a similar call on the afternoon William was dying. The call this morning is not a complete shock. For about a month my father has been gravely ill up in Michigan.

This morning, whatever happens, I know I wont go back to sleep. As I get up to make coffee while I make plans, I think back on the fifty years since my step-dad became my father.

He has been seriously ill with a variety of ongoing health issues since he retired in 1997. My mother, who has health problems of her own, has been taking care of him since that time.

Try as we might, the family could not convince them to move to Georgia. The last few years he has gotten considerably worse and has been constantly in and out of hospitals. He was born with an enlarged heart. His mother and younger brother both died from heart aliments.

For thirty years he worked long hours at one of the major auto manufacturers and held other side jobs to ensure that my mother, sister and I (as well as his three sons from a previous marriage) were provided for. He did his best to contribute to raising my sister and me in a Christian home.

He was never the mushy, sentimental, or talkative type of father. But we never doubted his love, which he showed by his actions, especially in providing for us.

It wasn't until he was older that Sherry and I felt comfortable telling him that we loved him. By then, he seemed at ease to say he loved us too. By now my sister and I are close with our father. Prior to this morning, we saw him six months ago on a visit to Detroit. I recall that visit as I sip coffee and wait for more news.

———————

In July of last year, the month after William died, my mother called to say that he wasn't doing well and was again admitted to the ICU. Sherry and I travel to Detroit.

At the hospital my father is weak but we are able to talk with him. His heart is weaker and he has problems with his kidneys. The second morning of our visit I sit in my mother's bedroom. I am upset because my father had not said one word to me about my husband or his death the month before.

I'm sure my mother mentioned something to him about it. Later that afternoon, after he is moved to a regular hospital room, my father asks to speak to my sister and me alone. He tells us how much he appreciates that we came to support our mother and that he loves us.

With sincerity, he says to me, "Sheila, I'm sorry I didn't say anything about William. I just didn't know what to say."

"But you could have said something, though," I reply.

My pain and stubbornness won't let him know I have already forgiven him. We hug him and tell him how much we love him. After a couple days we head back to Georgia.

————

The phone ringing brings my mind back to the present.

I simply say, "He's gone, isn't he?"

"Yes."

"I've booked a flight Sherry. Can you be here in an hour?"

"Are you ok Sheila?"

"Yes."

"Maybe I should call Dr. Charles or Dr. Olen. Do you really think you should be going through this again?

"Yes. We prepared for this a while ago. I am ok Sherry."

I go to therapy sessions once a week now. I tell my therapist, Dr. Olen, and psychiatrist, Dr. Charles, of the likelihood my father will die in the near future. Over the course of several sessions, we address my feelings and a plan for my care if it happens.

Neither doctor feels comfortable about me attending a funeral at this time. I am going through a season of constant nightmares and other symptoms which are developing as my mind lets in more memories, which I had blocked out since the trauma.

They suggest a phone conference with Sherry, who is with me constantly. She has also attended a session or two with me. They are familiar with our relationship and her concern for me. The purpose is to get her observations about my behavior.

Sherry admits that I am having a hard time of it lately, but tells them that most likely it would be even worse for me if I do not go to Detroit to be with my family in the event of my father's death.

After more consultation, I agree to the suggestion that Dr. Charles prescribe medication to ease the symptoms of panic attacks and to calm me as needed if the worst happens and I have to travel to Michigan.

However, we all agree that six months from William's death is far too soon for me to view my father's or any other corpse. Kim, who still lives up North, told us that my father's illness has taken a very unpleasant toll on his appearance. We come up with a compromise. I will be with the family and attend a memorial service but not view the body.

I have a fear of medicine because William's condition was caused by a reaction to medication. Because the medication prescribed is taken only as needed, I am not scared to take it to help me cope with all that is happening. I know that truthfully I need help to handle all that is going on with me in Georgia, let alone seeing my father lying in a casket right now. I fill the prescription and keep it on standby.

I fill the cat's food and water bowls. As I take the trash to the container on the patio, I look up at the clear black sky of this cold winter morning. There are stars everywhere. I think about my father and William as I gaze at the sky.

"Congratulations," I speak to them both, still looking up at the sky. "Take care of each other."

We arrive in Detroit a few hours later. My mother is upset and confused; unable to find paperwork and make arrangements for my father. His older son is at her home when we arrive; he's been with her since they left the hospital. We spend the day going through paperwork and making phone calls.

At one point my sister and step brother begin to look through old photographs from when we were all children. I see pictures of my parents and us kids. I feel like I am going to faint. Or scream. I have a strong adverse reaction to seeing the pictures from my past.

Seeing my expression, my step brother asks, "What's wrong?"

"I hate the past," is my snappy retort as I leave the room.

I want to fly back to Georgia right now. Instead, I take the first dose of medication prescribed by my psychiatrist. My father will be cremated following a memorial service. Against my better judgment, I include myself in the planning, even going to the funeral home to speak with the director. The medication keeps me reasonably even tempered.

At the service I see people I haven't seen in many years. I am numb and try to pretend this is happening to someone else. Afterward, I notice people going into the room in which my father's body lies. I take a step in that direction, drawn to the idea of seeing him one last time. Sherry blocks me and looks me in the eye.

"If you go in there I'm calling your doctor and never speaking to you again."

Her face is like a stone mask. I can't imagine what mine looks like for her to say those words to me. I head to the car and say goodbye to him silently in the back seat as we slowly drive through the icy streets toward my mother's house. I fly back home a few days later and pick up my life where I left off.

13 ISN'T SHE LOVELY?

It is 7:33 a.m.

I know this for sure because I take note of the time. I'm amazed as I watch my perfect, 7 pound 20 ounce healthy granddaughter enter this world. I push my way through the medical staff to get to the table where they get her vitals, weigh her, and suction her tiny nose and mouth.

I take a couple of pictures with my cell phone and send them to friends and family in Atlanta with the words "three minutes old" beneath them. She was born with her eyes open. They are still open and she is looking around the room, curious. I remember to start breathing again as I stand aside watching the staff attending to her.

I can't stop staring at the baby. The whole world fades away when her eyes meet mine (by accident, I think) and I bond with her and pledge to her a lifetime of love. She is my first grandchild. I have waited my whole life to see her. Nothing else matters, nothing is bigger than right now.

I tear myself away for a moment to go to Kim and Michael. I tell my daughter how beautiful the baby is and what a good job she did in delivery. Michael is crying with joy; he holds his wife's hand as they wait for the baby to be brought to the bed.

Trina has tears in her eyes as she talks to her sister. Kim is both elated and exhausted. Her labor was induced on Monday; today is Friday. The three of us have been at the hospital with Kim the entire week waiting for the baby to be delivered; Trina and I go to their apartment each night to sleep. Our fatigue is overshadowed by the happiness we feel.

I stay in the room a few minutes until the nurse tells us the baby will be going to the nursery to be cleaned up and tested. Trina and I go out to the waiting room where my ex-husband, Eugene, his sister, and the baby's paternal grandmother are waiting. I'm only slightly disappointed when they tell me they already knew that the baby had been born because Michael sent them a text.

A few minutes later I tell myself my disappointment is insensitive and possessive. The baby does not belong to me only just because Kim is my daughter. Everyone is as equally ecstatic as me. The moment passes and I'm happily celebrating the birth of "our girl" with everyone – smiles, hugs, and kisses fly around the waiting room.

For a time, I forget that we all spent the night right here in this waiting room, and for me it was not that easy.

———

I am all smiles and charm, as I 'hold court' with people that I've known for many years but have not seen recently. I am genuinely happy as we sit around making small talk and catching up on what I've missed since I moved away. We are an extended family and on one accord this evening waiting for the newest member to arrive.

Eugene knows I have PTSD. By now we are on good

terms. I have not seen him since Kim and Michael's wedding, though we talk occasionally. I appreciate that he was such a good friend to me when William died last year.

As usual, I'm terrified. But this night I have logical explanations for why my heart is pounding. My daughter is having her first child and her labor has been days long. Any number of things could go horribly wrong; as this family learned a little over a year ago.

I'm also tired physically because I am rest broken. I trust nothing or no one, including the staff at one of the best hospitals in the state of Michigan. I'm watching everything and everyone. I even have my eye on the ceiling beams in the waiting room. I'm satisfied they are sturdy.

Have I offended anyone? Is everyone happy? I check and recheck my words and actions through the night to ensure I've done nothing to create bad memories of this night for this loving band of well-wishers.

At around three in the morning, I recognize the signs that I'm going to get weird if I don't get somewhere by myself. The maternity waiting room is modern and roomy. I find a group of comfortable chairs around a corner, away from everyone. I pull two of them together and sit with my legs stretched out. I'm safe for now and no one is the wiser.

I hear Eugene's voice. "Sheila? Sheila? Oh, there she is, I see her legs."

I don't realize that my legs and feet can be seen through the small glass partition that separates the two waiting areas.

Dang! I've been spotted!

So I go back over to the group, smiling. I say that I was just taking a nap, which is a lie. I have never been able to sleep in a public place.

The expectant and excited group accepts my excuse for abandoning them and we spend the next couple of hours together waiting.

————

A few hours later a nurse tells us we can go to the nursery and see the baby. We jump up, excited, and make our way down the corridor. We ring the buzzer at the entrance to the nursery. Another nurse appears from behind the door and one of us tells her who we are there to see.

She says, "It has not gone as planned. You cannot see her now."

The hallway is in a rapid, dizzying tailspin, and then I am at the hospital in Atlanta where William died. It looks the same as the year before. The smell is also the same. The nurse is telling me my husband is dying and I cannot see him now. The room dims and I begin to pass out.

I hear my former sister in law say, "Catch her."

Someone keeps me from falling to the floor. I become aware of where I am and that it is not William in a room somewhere behind those doors. I look into the eyes of the tall nurse. Now I'm fearful for my granddaughter.

"Is something is wrong with her?" I ask. My voice sounds too loud in my ears.

The nurse reassures us that she is fine; it is just taking longer to draw her blood. We are told to go back to the waiting room and we will be called when we can see the baby.

With my heart still pounding, I assure everyone I am fine. They are concerned and encourage me to eat something. Their concern means the world to me.

I say that I think the last nurse could have chosen her words better, knowing any family is concerned about their new baby. They all agree. I am relieved they don't know the impact the exchange had on me. I don't want to be the weakest link.

In a short time we are escorted to the baby. One peek and I fall in love all over again. She's swaddled in a blanket and appears to be fine. We all take more pictures and tell her she's beautiful and how much she's loved.

For now, the flashback is forgotten in the joy of this moment. I will think about it another day. I will try to remember to mention the episode to the doctor when I'm back in Georgia.

The wonderful day goes by quickly. I'm grateful that Trina had the chance to visit with her niece; she has to return to work. Her flight back to Georgia is tonight.

The baby's mom and dad are ecstatic. I am honored

to be there with them. I field phone calls and texts from other family members and from good friends who are delighted for us. They enjoy calling me "Granny". If only they knew what a badge of honor that name is for me.

I get to hold the baby doll a lot today. Although it has been many years since I've held a newborn, it's like riding a bike - not easy to forget when that "new baby" smell hits my nose. Now its evening and I have to leave the hospital so that the parents can spend time together with their baby and I can get some rest.

Like I can rest.

I thank God that everything went well with my family this time. This is one of the most fantastic days of my entire life.

14 SEASON OF BITTER DARKNESS

During this season, an oppressive, unmoving, and relentless heaviness covers me like a second skin. It smothers me, it's debilitating and it's mean to the core. Today my sister has come with me to run several errands. We are on the freeway driving towards my home.

"I really don't give a damn anymore!" I say suddenly.

"About what?"

"Living."

I have developed a habit of starting conversations in my head and then finishing them out loud. My statement was the end such a dialogue. The words spilled from my lips.

Although it was not my intent to include Sherry in what I had been thinking before I spoke, one thing is crystal clear to me. I have never spoken more truthfully than I have in this very moment. I'm done with all of this.

Even though we are not looking at each other, I feel Sherry recoil at my words. She knows me more than anyone and I think my words have shocked and hurt her deeply. I stubbornly refuse to take them back, even when she does her best to encourage me as we ride along. I sense that she is heartbroken and weary. I can feel her heartache; she senses that her little sister is giving up.

A part of me is relieved that she knows. Now she

won't have the burden of working so hard to help me deal with the ugliness. I desperately want her, and everyone else, to just let me sink to the bottom of the murky seas which hold my destiny. It will be a relief for everyone, especially me. That's what I really believe lately.

I imagine myself telling her how much I admire her. She is brave and strong, not just for me, but her entire family. Right now though, I am neither able nor willing to express how much I love, respect and appreciate her. It takes too much effort.

Instead, I embrace the rage and the next thing I know cannot stop myself from saying too much. I reveal to her that I am furious with God for letting William die, especially in that manner. It seems as if I have fallen off the edge of the cliff this time.

I have selfishly pushed my sister to the limit with this dismaying revelation. She's done all she can. She is also in mourning, tired, and afraid. And for her time and trouble today, I have rewarded her with my outburst. I'm some sister.

Real or imagined, I believe she has become impatient with me. I am confused; maybe she isn't. But I wouldn't blame her if she is.

Possibly, she is simply feeling helpless. Maybe she just wants to finish the day with her family in peace without worrying about me. I don't know. I tell her to just get me home so I can take medication to calm me and to get some sleep. She gets me home and talks with me until I am able to doze off.

I wonder if I'm schizophrenic. The doctors say I'm not. Then how am I alive and, simultaneously, dead? How can I laugh so heartily at the same time my soul is bitterly weeping? I do thank and praise God for the things he provides. Then the next moment, I'm wounded and angry He allowed this to happen. I feel two-faced toward God, and guilty.

In the bible, the man Job told his wife:

"Thou speakest as one of the foolish women speaketh. What? Shall we receive good at the hand of God, and shall we not receive evil?" (Job 2:10 KJV)

The verse continues to read that in all of his troubles Job did not sin by speaking against God. Unlike Job, I can't seem to accept this tragedy; even though my loss cannot compare to those Job suffered. I roll my eyes when I think of the irony that this was a scripture my husband frequently quoted.

I don't understand that He would allow such a horrible thing to happen to a man who had such faith in Him.

Then I realize I am only able to function each day in this pit of darkness because He is performing such a miracle. Thinking about it all gives me a headache. I retreat to my bed and refuse to try to make sense of it. Sometimes for days at a time.

My mood is stable as I sit across from Dr. Olen this morning. As usual, we exchange pleasantries and then get down to business. I haven't seen her for a month or so. She asks what has been going on lately.

"Among other things, I was admitted to the hospital since I last saw you. The doctors thought I had a stroke."

Concerned, she asks, "What happened?"

I decide to give her the short version.

"It started as a headache for two days that was so severe I went to the emergency room. I was given Morphine and told I had a virus and sent home. For four days the headache and other symptoms got worse."

She stops typing notes on the computer and I continue.

"I returned to the hospital and was admitted to the Stroke Unit because I was in and out of consciousness and incapable of speaking coherently. I didn't even know my own name or the car I drive."

As it turned out, the virus had depleted the sodium and potassium in my body to the extent that my brain and central nervous symptoms were temporarily affected."

I tell her that I was brought back to health within a few days and released. She asks how I feel about the experience.

"What bothered me is that the medical staff who spoke with me kept referring to the mental health related notations in my charts.

They asked me questions about what happened with my husband. They inquired how I was feeling emotionally just as often as how I was doing physically."

"Why did that bother you Sheila?" I don't realize I'm frowning and my voice is slightly raised.

"Because they kept taking notes and probing into what I was thinking and feeling; asking was I depressed, suicidal, stuff like that.

At one point they sent a psychiatrist in to talk to me about the PTSD and depressive symptoms I experience."

"What did you discuss with this doctor?"

"Not much. I explained that I had a psychiatrist and therapist that I saw on a regular basis; which is in my medical chart."

I begin to get agitated again.

"Can you tell me what it is that bothered you so much? Did you think they were neglecting your physical care?"

"I believe they addressed my physical needs. But I felt as though they were trying to make a case that I needed to be admitted to the psychiatric ward of the hospital when I was well enough.

William's illness and death and my subsequent mental breakdown are not what landed me in the hospital, it was a physical concern. I felt like they were gathering information for some type of experiment, or worse."

She waits until I calm my breathing and I continue.

"I was afraid. They asked detailed questions about William's death, and whether I was still depressed. I explained that yes, he died and of course I am depressed. Not only about his death, but because I am so sick and my youngest daughter is terrified I'm going to die too.

I felt like they could just treat my physical problems and let me get home and continue my sessions."

"I can tell the experience upset you. I am sorry. How do you feel about it now?"

We talk for a while about the hospital experience. I am finally able to express that part of my problem was that it was the first time I felt stigmatized for my mental health condition. I was also afraid that I would go into an episode and they wouldn't let me go home.

I decide to step out from the comfort of some sense of privacy and tell this woman that my spiritual beliefs have been damaged. The same Christian who ministered to hurting women for years is now so deeply hurt she cannot function spiritually.

She listens patiently as I tell her that I feel betrayed by God. Then, on the heels of that feeling, I'm immensely guilty because I should know better. How dare I be ungrateful after all He has done for me?

I wrestle with even trying to talk to the God I loved

and been loved by for many years. That scowling, gray Jehovah that I envisioned as a teenager surely would not accept such behavior.

But the loving God who sent His Son to die for me understands I have been deeply wounded. I know that but can't feel it. Even if He still loves me, is my faith so damaged that I will not be able to trust Him again?

I am surprised that my confession did not seem to surprise her. She tells me that what I felt was not uncommon. Rather, it is a real reaction to a trauma of the magnitude I had experienced. Like many people who are hurting, I was striking out (and blaming) the one closest to me.

She is right on that point. My faith has been blasted into oblivion with the force of a fifty-eight megaton bomb. Though my faith is in pieces, my belief is unscathed. I still know that He is, was, and is to come.

We confirm our next appointment to discuss this matter further. As I leave the office, the heavens didn't part to reveal the answers I was seeking. Nor did lightening strike me dead. It occurs to me that I hadn't told the therapist anything God didn't know already. My soul is slightly lifted.

———

During this season of ingratitude, unhappiness and fury, I am reminded that God is still merciful. I suppose that I would deserve it if He destroyed me for allowing my anger at Him to rage so hot that I get close to committing blasphemy.

At the same time another part of me thinks about His love and forgiveness whether I am happy, depressed, or simply existing. I go back and forth between these two perspectives day after dark day.

Now and then I pick up the bible. In no way do I study the scriptures daily or as diligently as I had in the past. But sometimes I feel the need to read a verse or two.

This morning I pick up the bible on my nightstand. As I lift it, I get a feeling of separation from my Savior. I bring the bible to my lips and kiss it.

I say aloud, "I miss You." Meaning God.

I miss the comfort of my relationship with Him, just as I do my husband. I lie back on the bed on my side and hold the bible without opening its pages. I close my eyes and don't speak. About half an hour passes and I open my eyes. My pillow is soaked with tears.

Gradually, but not regularly, I am beginning to pray in addition to just saying grace at mealtime. Sometimes I talk to Him and question why He allowed William to die like he did.

Other times I resent Him for what happened; almost demanding He tell me what was the point and purpose for giving, then taking away, the gift He gave me.

Maybe I have always been insane. Wouldn't that be something?

"I know and understand what you feel. If I were human I would be angry too. But I'm not human. And I know what's best. Trust Me."

This inaudible but real message I heard the other day struck a chord of bare truth within me. In essence, it confirmed what I had been taught about God and his omnipotence. He has no limits. William was His son from before he was born.

Over the years I will tell many people about this message from God. They agree with me that it is in agreement with what the Bible says. But though my mind knows the words are true, these days I stubbornly reject His decision. I harbor a measure and mistrust of not only God, but of everything in life. If He allowed this to happen, all bets are off. Nothing and no one is safe.

I am terrified of the known and unknown; constantly afraid that more tragedy is lurking nearby at all times.

Slowly, cautiously, I am peeking around a spiritual corner. I miss going to church, but I am unable to return to our former church. Within several services after the funeral, I realized that being there upset me more than it fortified me spiritually. The memories are beyond painful and too vivid to ignore.

I found a small church near my home that I am attending. The pastor and his wife are loving and kind. They teach the scriptures accurately and enthusiastically. They welcome me with open arms. One Saturday night I call them to ask could I meet with them privately after church on Sunday.

At the meeting I explained that I had PTSD and the basics of the circumstances that caused the condition. They are surprised.

I ask if they had ever ministered to anyone with this or other mental illness. They honestly tell me that they have not. But they reassure me that they will research the condition and will support and minister to me with all their might. I don't have a single doubt they will do just that.

A few months have passed. To a large extent I enjoy the comfort of being part of a church family again. Even so, I have no intention of becoming a member of this or any other church. I don't feel I can handle the stress of being obligated to attend and participate, neither am I ready to let my "secret" out in the open.

I am afraid I will be called upon to again share my spiritual gifts and talents here. I don't know why that prospect bothers me, but it does. Probably just me being selfish or scared.

———

More time has passed. I've gradually, deliberately pulled myself away from the tiny church family. The pastor and his wife keep their word and do not pressure me into coming to church. Eventually, they give me the space I am so obviously seeking and stop contacting me. I'm relieved and a bit sad at the same time.

I think about the loving couple who tried so hard to welcome and love me. I ran away. I didn't know if they would understand my instability and inability to maintain consistent behaviors and meet deadlines of any sort.

Over the course of several sessions I share these events with Dr. Olen. She reminds me how some people with PTSD absolutely cannot tolerate the pressure of being needed or meeting even the smallest deadlines.

I have found therapy to be one of several life-saving methods to obtaining wholeness. I'm able to openly reveal everything on my mind without hurting, shocking or offending the therapist.

It's hard to tell people I love everything in my heart, mind, and soul because it touches and affects them deeply. I've told them more than I should have as it is. But then, if I did not have the love and support of the people who know me personally therapy would be meaningless.

Though she and Dr. Charles listen and accept my realities, they constantly guide me to find avenues to combat the terrors and untruths which plague me on a daily basis.

We spend numerous sessions identifying things that are real and separating them from emotions like fear or anxiety, which are only feelings that can't do me harm.

They reinforce that there are no "normal" ways to fight PTSD; each patient's symptoms and treatment are unique. In my case, at least for now, we have developed a treatment plan which consists of behavioral therapy in addition to medication for treatment of severe panic and anxiety attacks. I'm also given sleep aids as needed, since my symptoms increase when I have the bouts of insomnia. I control my options and choose when it is time to cease or refuse certain treatments.

I'm learning exercises to do at home, such as controlling my breathing and making deliberate efforts to control my thinking. Sometimes I am successful with doing my homework. Most of the time I am not able to try. But even when I won't or can't, even if it's for a week or two, I am getting more consistent with getting myself back on track.

———

The Christmas 2012 holiday season has arrived. Unlike last year, I want no part of it whatsoever. I am puzzled by the resistance to enjoying the holidays this year. I'm also depressed as all get out. This same time last year was the first holiday season after his death and I celebrated it fully. Go figure.

I decide to visit my new granddaughter in Detroit this year. Every time I think of her I smile. I hold on to the upcoming visit like a lifeline. My flight leaves tonight.

After saying goodbye to Trina at the airport, I board the plane and realize my seat is over the wing of the aircraft. For all the years I have flown I've carefully avoided seats in this section. This time I purchased the seat online and didn't bother to check where it was located.

Today, I honestly do not care. The plane is crowded

and noisy. As the plane prepares to ascend, engine noise and the loud voices of passengers talking over the noise assault my ears. I feel the vibration of the engine in my feet. I look out of the window and all I see is the wing of the plane. *So what?*, I say to my disinterested self.

My affect is flat, as they say in the mental health profession. The aircraft turns. It tilts sideways and I can see the city parallel with the ground. I don't feel fear or anything else.

I boldly look out at the world, which is askew from this vantage point. I want just one thing for Christmas-please. And that is that this plane crashes. Hard.

Stop it right now! I replace this thought with the image of my granddaughter. I thank God for not granting my Christmas wish and I'm in Detroit within a couple of hours.

I'm cheerful in the company of my loving family for the next several days. We pack all the fun we can into my visit. The baby is even more beautiful than the pictures they sent me.

I enjoy spending time with her alone while her parents run errands. I talk in her ear a lot, telling how much I love her. Her scent is the unmistakable odor of baby shampoo and joyful love. I inhale deeply to save the smell in my memory to savor when I go back home.

I'm going home today. I am ready to return to the safety of my own bedroom. The weather reports that a severe snowstorm is headed this way. It slams full force on our way to the airport.

I spend hours delayed at the airport. This is not really a problem for me; I've always liked airports and watching people go to and fro to various destinations. A couple of hours ago I had a nice dinner and now I'm settled in with a good book.

Suddenly, I feel anxious in the crowded airport. I take half a dose of anxiety medicine; enough to calm but not impair me.

We are finally boarded and the plane is de-iced. I arrive back in Atlanta in one piece. I'm glad to be back at home without real incident. The pictures from the trip uplift my spirits over the next couple of months. By early spring, I'm finding bright spots here and there. My moods are stabilizing more quickly when I get upset.

I read once that there are a few different ways that sharks feed. Some sharks feed through their filters, others shred their food and then devour it. There are still other sharks that hunt their prey and quickly gulp it down in one whole piece.

At times like these I feel like insanity is the shark that is trying to swallow me in a single gulp. The good news for me is that it is unsuccessful because I keep struggling against such a fate.

I keep remembering that success may be mine some day.

15 THE UNCOMFORTABLE ZONE

A pleasant rapport has developed between the therapist and I since we first met a year and a half ago. As I sit in her clean, quiet office today I do feel a measure of discomfort. But it is not because I mistrust her expertise or question her confidentiality, like when I first began treatment.

"How are things going, Sheila?"

"It has been a while since I've been in. But I made this particular appointment because the suicidal thoughts have returned."

"Has something happened that upset you? How were the holidays for you?"

I fill her in on the challenges I faced the during this holiday season. I explain that I am confused that I am in worse shape than the same time the previous year. She asks why I am frowning.

I can't seem to pull my thoughts together so I can express what I'm feeling. I say that I believe I should get better as more time passes. I feel as if I am going backward rather than forward.

My voice catches in my throat as I'm speaking. The worst part of this illness for me is when I do good for a while, and then suddenly plunge into the depths of depression.

When I come up for air, Dr. Olen says she would like to remind me of a few things before we move on.

"That ordeal, contrary to what you may feel, was not that long ago Sheila. As you cope with the trauma, you are also still grieving the loss of your husband.

As I told you, there is no timetable when you 'should' be better."

I nod my head and try to absorb what she is once again telling me.

"Your father died around this same time last year, didn't he?"

I answer in the affirmative. She watches me closely as I process the implication of her question. She encourages me to recognize that I am also still grieving for my father. I agree to the possibility.

For the next few minutes she addresses the grief aspect of what I'm feeling, confirming its validity. I talk about my father, not just his death, but who he was as a person. Then she returns to the subject of the panic attacks.

"Try to tell me what you are thinking or feeling just before your alarm and sadness reach their highest point."

"It depends. Sometimes I'm not thinking of anything specific at all."

She waits for me to complete my thought.

"Other times I am feeling abandoned, scared, or lonely, Dr. Olen."

Then she asks, "And do you have physical symptoms?"

"Yes. My heart races and I get sweaty and shaky. I have difficulty breathing. I feel like I'm dying."

"Those are symptoms of panic attacks, remember?"

She reminds me how to recognize the symptoms of panic attacks and gives me more literature with new information about them.

I'm relieved she doesn't show signs of impatience because she has told me these things repeatedly. Though I understand, it is hard for me to recall what I've learned when I'm in the midst of panic or depression. Once again, I commit to remind myself that there's no real threat during the attacks and to keep reading the literature and doing the exercises.

After discussing any other potential triggers and confirming the plan of action for my treatment, the session ends. I take away several points from this visit. Dr. Olen affirms that I am making progress.

I feel empowered to some degree. On the other hand, I am scared because I am starting to realize how complex and lengthy the process of healing will be. I probably still have a very long road ahead of me. The doctor encourages me to stop being hard on myself.

There are so many layers to work through. I'm

starting to feel overwhelmed; so I'm relieved when the session ends. I confirm our next appointment.

16 IT GETS DEEPER

My schedule includes therapy sessions in addition to psychiatrist, medical doctor, dentist, and eye doctor appointments. Sometimes I cancel one or the other if they are too close together in the week so that I don't have to leave home alone more than two times a week.

Today the appointment is with the psychiatrist, Dr. Charles. He is a very soft spoken and calm man. I wonder if his demeanor is rehearsed; part of a deliberate strategy psychiatrists use to keep people like me from getting too agitated. I'm usually untroubled when I'm here. I sometimes break down and cry when I try to answer some of his questions, though.

I am "dressed appropriately", as they write in doctor's notes, as I walk into his office. I remember that during my last visit with him I cried a lot. I had difficulty making eye contact and I looked out the large windows in his office, wondering why I bothered to come. He suggested we develop new strategies for coping with trauma and its symptoms during this visit.

Today, I feel embarrassed. I walk past the doctor into his office.

"Good morning Sheila. You look nice today."

"Thank you." *I bet you say that to all the nut cases.*

He waits until I am seated before he sits behind his

desk.

"How are you today?"

I never know how to answer this question when people ask me. If I say "fine", most people take me at face value and accidentally overwhelm me with chitchat, social invitations, or their own problems.

If I say, "not so good", there are times when I get sympathy, pity or some unwanted advice on how to feel better. Sometimes I can't see how anyone would want to be around me with all of my complexities.

I avoid the doctor's question with a sigh and shrug of the shoulders. Then I deliberately bring my gaze to meet his eyes. Because he is a professional, I am assuming he is not expecting an answer from me one way or another.

His fingers are poised to begin typing as we talk. Mine are tapping the wooden arm of the chair. I hope my purse is covering my hand. I've learned how to tap with the balls of my fingers when I'm around other people. I'm determined to remain positive today. After all, I have been in therapy a year and a half so I should have made some progress.

"How has your therapy been going?" he asks.

"I have been going regularly and it has helped some."

My answer is intentionally evasive. I'm being cautious. I still don't know if what I say or do can be used to make a case that I should be committed to a hospital.

I'm concentrating hard to think of positive things to talk about. Then, out of nowhere, I start spilling my guts out, once again, about what happened to William. Like he doesn't know the story.

He's listening but in my mind he wants to move on to something else. I could kick myself for speaking negatively. When I take a breath he asks me to tell him what I am currently experiencing.

I explain how I thought I was grieving normally after my husband died until the obsessive tapping, nightmares, insomnia, panic attacks, intense fear, suicidal ideations, and other behaviors took over my life. *He has your chart, he consults with Dr. Olen, and you've seen him for a year, remember Sheila?*

I slow my breathing and start again. He wants to hear from me, in my own words, what I'm going through right now.

I tell him how I still cannot find my way back to my relationship with God. I tell him that it is impossible for me to go back to the church William and I served in so faithfully. The doctor nods his head for me to continue as he writes notes in the computer.

"I constantly go over the details of how he died."

The doctor reacts with a slight expression of sorrow on his face. Then he switches gears and asks me a series of questions. For about ten minutes I answer questions about where I live now, who lives with me, and my support system. He wants to know what brought my husband and me to Georgia.

He asks about my daughters and I perk up a bit and talk about them. He inquires about their relationship with William. I tell him that they were close to their stepfather.

We spend the next few minutes discussing the relationship between me and my deceased husband. Ours was a solid, basically happy marriage. I am also forthright that it was far from perfect. At some point my eyes follow a tear that traveled from my chin and plopped onto my purse. I wonder when that happened; my voice didn't sound tearful to my ears.

I don't know what I could have done or said, but now he's asking me if I have firearms in the house. *What?!*

I tell him that I don't.

I think, *I bet if I really wanted to kill myself, right now I would use my own hands.*

Sarcasm is alive and well in the twisted mind of Sheila Kay. I must be getting better.

Toward the end he asks questions related to my medication and future treatment plans. I have grown to appreciate the doctor's tranquil temperament and evident professionalism.

Then he's refilling my prescriptions and making our next appointment. I'm not at all angry but my eyebrows are knit together and my lips are a straight line on my face. We say goodbye and I walk to the elevators.

It wasn't until I get in my car that I ponder whether I didn't know I was crying because I was tapping. Damn!

Well anyway, I've got to get home now before somebody tries to kill me in this parking lot. I start the car.

17 PERMISSION GRANTED

I wake up suddenly in the middle of the night and throw the covers from my body. The room is dark except for the illumination from the lamppost outside on the curb. I can hear the hum of the furnace and, although my sleep is broken again, I feel unusually peaceful and calm in the quiet darkness.

I am keenly aware the time has come to begin writing about my journey. I'm not shocked or afraid because the idea has been a tiny seed in my heart and mind for a few years.

Now it is alright, in fact, necessary, for me to open up about what happened. I see this with crystal clarity.

God knows I am afraid that writing the gruesome details will be detrimental to my progress. Nevertheless, I know the time has come. It may even be helpful for me to write, as Dr. Olen once suggested to me.

Kenneth is a man with whom I have been in a committed relationship with for about a year and a half at this point. He is a hard working, strong, Christian man four years older than me. Having survived his own problems in life, he is understanding and accepting of my struggles. I appreciate that he challenges me, even though I resist him in so many ways.

As he puts it, he's just waiting on me to say the word so we can marry one day. I'm hardly ready to take that step, but I am grateful for his companionship and support.

I tell Kenneth about the epiphany. He is well aware that I have been considering writing the book for years.

"I think you should do it. No, I know you should do it. It will be a best seller. You are an excellent writer, Sheila."

"You think so? Yeah, I think so too." I smile at my modesty.

His words are not mere flattery. He knows me very well and has read a great deal of my writing and editing.

"Kenneth you know me. I would rather be rich than popular. I ghostwrite and edit because it feels more private to me."

"I believe that you are put here on earth to share your gifts. You are going to be on The Bill Maher show."

He chuckles. Mr. Maher is his favorite political comedian but he knows I'm not a fan.

I roll my eyes. *Bill Maher. Very funny.*

I let both my daughters know that I will begin writing my story. They affirm and encourage me, but I sense hesitancy in their words, probably because of their concern for me. Or it could be I'm reading too much into what people say and do yet again. No surprise there.

I have become paranoid; even in small matters it is hard for me to trust in a positive outcome. Sometimes it causes problems between me and Kenneth. The best I can do is to keep trying, even as I make the effort to trust myself.

About a week later I tell Sherry that I have been released to begin writing. I let her know that most likely the William and his condition will be central within a complete autobiography. She is also a writer. I value her opinion as well as her friendship and loyalty.

Sherry is excited about the book and offers advice and ideas. She openly expresses her concerns about the effect the writing will have on me and cautions me to take care of myself. We have a long enjoyable conversation about my new venture and about the new book she is working on currently.

My mind is all over the place. So much has happened. I'm undecided about how much or how little to include in the book. From the start, I know the opening scene will take place on that day I had the breakdown in the medical doctor's office. This idea wouldn't go away, so I will follow my instincts.

I've finished the fledgling draft of the opening scene. It tells what happened, but I'm not happy with it when I read it aloud. It reads as if I am an observer or reporting the incident. The point of the book is to relate the story from the inside.

After a few days of thinking it over, I decide to write in the first person, using "*I*" this or that, instead of "*she*". After the first rewrite of that chapter, I am satisfied this point of view will bring the reader closer to me as I go through my journey. So it is from this viewpoint I write and take notes going forward. I am telling the story as seen through my eyes. I still haven't decided in what order to put the events. It doesn't concern me, though; I can make that decision later.

———

Initially, I am sure I should base the book around the disease, Toxic Epidermal Necrolysis (TEN), which eventually killed William. Besides the medical personnel caring for him, I was the closest person to him during the last thirteen days of his life. I witnessed the effects of the dreadful disease up close and personal.

I couple of years ago I rejected the suggestion of Eye Movement Desensitization and Reprocessing (EMDR), a therapy which is used to treat some combat PTSD survivors. I learned that part of the process involved repeating the worst of the trauma, and I knew I could not handle the stress it would place upon me.

I consider the reasons for that decision as I prepare to write the book. Writing about TEN in detail will most likely put my unstable mental health at risk. I'm rethinking my decision.

How do I remain true to my conviction to write and maintain a balance between true events and exploitation of the gory details I witnessed? I conclude that I should just tell my whole story, from my point of view.

Now my voyage begins.

I have handwritten notes all over the house with things I want to include within the book. But as it turns out, when I open my laptop to start writing, I begin the book with an outpouring of acknowledgement and thanks rather than the biographical information I had been jotting down.

As I begin typing, the immense love and gratitude I feel toward family, friends, supporters, and God flow like a river from the tips of my fingers, transforming into words on a white page.

The dam that has been holding back my tears for the day suddenly bursts. I keep typing, barely able to see the screen. In my mind's eye I see the faces of my family as they appeared when they stood beside me during the worse time of my life.

The actual writing of the book isn't pretty. The scene does not reflect the romance novel author preparing to entice his readers. Nor does it portray the sophistication of a scholarly writer poised to put pen to paper. When I'm done, my face is wet, my eyes red, and my face contorted. The moment is raw and genuine. I feel like I am dying...or being born. Or both.

When I am done with the draft of the acknowledgements, I am satisfied that the people I love will know how I feel about them. I save the document and close the computer.

———

Over the next couple of months, in between other

writing projects, I complete drafts of a chapter or two. There's no chronological order at this point, I write in fits and starts about whatever comes to my mind.

One night I write of the last time William and I attend church together; another day I relate what led up to taking him to the hospital. I pull out some of the printouts of my doctor's appointment summaries so I can create a compilation to include somewhere in the book. I follow what pops in my head.

At this point I'm not sure what I will cut from the final draft. I am excited and proud that I have been given the strength to even begin the daunting project.

In the meantime, I live day by day. When I'm not writing, my time is spent with Kenneth and my family. I have changed since tragedy. But everyone, including me, has been willing and able to make adjustments. I am flawed but I am needed nonetheless, and it makes me feel good.

There is freedom in not being scared to reveal my imperfections. Every human being owns a unique set of faults. I'm no better or worse. I set aside my pride more easily and accept support and advice without feeling I'm being pitied or criticized. I am valued and I know it.

I even dare to believe that despite my illness, some people actually admire me for who I am and have become. I'm starting to pray and read my bible again. I'm not ready to join a church yet, but my spirit feels reconnected.

———

I am at a standstill writing the book. Lately, I am unable to complete chapters or tie ideas together cohesively. I chalk up the writer's block to the book's disturbing subject matter; namely TEN. I struggle with telling my story without exploiting William or appearing self depreciating. It is also important to me that I make it clear that I identify as a conqueror, not victim.

Yesterday, it came to me that maybe there are two books to the story. The main focus of the first book should be on William, our lives, marriage and ministry, and his subsequent death from TEN. Later, I would write a smaller book about my experience living with PTSD.

So I have begun to write again and as I do, the subject keeps coming back to my life with PTSD. Soon I find myself hoping the book will translate into awareness of Post Traumatic Stress Disorder from the standpoint of an ordinary, unknown woman.

I can't imagine what it was like for William to be tortured by TEN, and he did not live long enough to share his experience. But I live daily with PTSD. I can give the subject life and realism from an insider's perspective. I'm still unsure that PTSD should be the book's focal point.

This winter morning I sit looking out at the gray sky and leafless trees. I ask myself if I can trust what I'm hearing from my subconscious mind: There should be only one book, that is, one biographical book.

It makes sense to me somehow. I sip coffee as I turn over the idea in my head.

I will write just one book about everything. The subject will be Sheila Kay. It will be a memoir, in fact. The story of who, what, when, where, and how I arrived at this moment in time. Telling the whole story will capture the both the dramatic and mundane moments of my life up to, including, and after William's death.

Having made a final decision, it takes a few more weeks to strategize how I can reuse some of what I have already written and incorporate it into a new book. During this time I have come to grips with even more issues that I have been hesitant to admit, as well as more memories have surfaced.

For instance, I must accept that I have been feeling humiliated because I no longer have control of my mental faculties. Following that, I have to accept that I never have had control of my mental faculties, or anything else. God is The Controller. I've spoken those words thousands of times, but the events of the past few years have brought them home to me.

These thoughts bring me to accepting that, as The One who knows and controls all things, He allowed the things in my life to happen. And if I believe that (and I do) then He will decide the direction and eventuality of this book.

———

My closest friend from the former church calls and leaves messages every now and then. For over two years I have avoided her, although I send her a text now and then. She is lovingly persistent. When she called and left a message last summer I returned her call and we talked briefly.

It is a couple days before Christmas and she is calling again. I decide to answer her call. She is overjoyed when I answer on the second ring. I feel a twinge of guilt for avoiding her for so long.

I am smiling as I listen to her familiar voice. I still have the ability to make her laugh, and her giggle takes me back to happier times. I keep the subject matter of the conversation superficial. *Don't say too much. It will be all over the church as soon as you hang up.*

"It is so good to speak with you. I wondered what I had done that you would stop talking to me," she tells me.

"You have done nothing. You were with me through the whole ordeal. I have always loved you and always will…"

I stop in the middle of the sentence. I was going to finish by simply saying I have not been feeling well, which is, in fact, an understatement. But just leaving it at that is hypocritical and simplistic. It won't make sense if she doesn't know about my ongoing illness. She will assume I had a passing physical ailment.

I decide to tell her the truth.

"I might as well tell you. I have PTSD."

I wait for her reaction. She is a nurse and she knows the implications of what I have said to her. I ask her to please keep what I am going to tell her in confidence.

"Oh, no my sister. I am so sorry. What happened?" she asks.

I hear her love and concern as she speaks. But she is confused. "You came back to church right afterward."

"Right. Later that year I started acting and thinking really strangely. Since that time I have been under the care of mental health professionals as well as my regular doctors."

My friend listens quietly as I tell her some of the details of what led to my diagnosis. I know that she is saddened by the news. I also know her well enough to be pretty sure she's not an advocate of mental health care or medication, like many Christians. Yet I've never known her to be judgmental.

I believe that God can use any means, including supernatural, doctors, and/or medications to heal those He loves, something I've said many times. It occurs to me that I may have chosen not to tell my former church members out of concern for their reaction to me getting mental health treatment.

I open up to her why coming back to the church was difficult. As the months went by, I tell her, even the smell of our church caused me physical discomfort and left me emotionally exhausted. I could see and hear William in my mind during the services, it was so painful.

For weeks I wondered why I would shake and cry each time I drove to and from the church. She patiently listens as I reveal that I eventually made the connection that the church is next door to the funeral home that handled William's final arrangements.

His body went from the hospital in Atlanta to the funeral home, then just across the parking lot to the church for his memorial service. Finally, his remains were buried at a cemetery not far away. To this day I never go close to that part of the city.

After I tell her as much of the truth as I care to, I start to feel like a weight has been lifted from my heart. My smile gets bigger by the minute.

We catch up on the state of our families; it surprises us that four years have passed. We briefly reminisce about the times we served together at church. The conversation lasts about an hour.

I deliberately make no promise to stay in touch or get together for a visit to avoid hurting her feelings. I still need some time. I don't know how long it will be before I'm ready to pick up our friendship where we left off, or forge a new relationship in light of what has occurred.

Right now I'm content that I have taken the huge step of confiding in her. But we do promise to text photos of each other's grandchildren.

I am relaxed and smiling as I look at her grandchildren's pictures on my phone a few minutes after we hang up. My concern about who she tells has vanished in the wind.

I tell Kenneth about the conversation. His eyebrow

raises slightly, an expression I've come to know as the "are you alright?" look, but he says nothing.

"I'm fine."

Christmas music is playing softly. I send a few pictures to my friend.

18 SIGNS OF PROGRESS

Today I get the chance to spend time alone with my granddaughter. Her parents are out for some time alone together. I used to watch her often, besides seeing her at family outings on weekends. Now that her mother is working from home I don't see the baby as much.

I look at her walking around in my kitchen after having a forty-five second meltdown when her dad leaves.

"Where's Georgia, Grammy?"

Just like that. Tantrum over.

My ten year old grey cat walks into the kitchen. She was named Georgia by my husband and me because we got her as we were preparing to move from Detroit. My granddaughter adores Georgia with all her heart.

"Oh, there she is!"

She rubs the cat's head. I have taught the baby not to rub Georgia's hindquarters. I tell her it huts the cat, but it actually just irritates the heck out of Georgia to be touched below her waist. She is, after all, a lady.

The toddler beams. "Soft," she says.

Georgia tolerates the interaction for about a minute, she's used to the enthusiastic attention. Then she makes her way over to the food bowl to have her breakfast. My granddaughter is satisfied with sharing the brief moment of bonding. She looks around, ready to move on to something more exciting than Georgia gobbling down her kibble.

My eyes are stinging. But these tears are different from the ones I used to shed because of fear that my mental illness would prevent me from being a good grandmother. Those tears dried up some time ago.

These are the tears parents and grandparents shed as they watch their little ones become healthy, independent beings. They fall from my eyes down to my smile, leaving a trail of joy and thankfulness.

I turn from her and quickly wipe my face. I look at her but I'm not smiling as usual, lost in the moment of gratitude.

"What's wrong Grammy?"

My face lights up. "Nothing's wrong baby."

And I mean it.

"Sit up here, Grammy?"

She points to the countertop; she's asking me to let her sit on it. I remember when she was much smaller and would sit on the counter watching me cook. I lift her to the counter with her back against the backsplash.

"Hi, mixer. Hi other mixer. Hi bowl," she says excitedly.

She has always been fascinated with my assortment of

mixers, food processor, blender, and other small appliances on the countertop. She calls them all "mixer", probably because they are all stainless steel and look similar. Kim says she's the same in her kitchen.

That's her cue for me to will find something we can cook together.

I listen to her happy chatter. She puts entire sentences of two and three syllable words together. Today's she's saying words that I haven't heard her say before, even though it has been just eight days since I saw her.

I understand most of what she says. As we talk, I again see how bright she is. From the day she was born, she's been a happy, laughing child. She's two and a half now, a little girl more than baby. Her legs are longer and more slender. She is beautiful inside and out. I don't have an ounce of guilt for spoiling her.

I am relieved of feeling ashamed that I am not "whole". I'm confident I can be a positive influence in her life despite (and because of) what I have conquered. When I'm with her PTSD is a distant relative.

We have another good day together. I'm a happy kind of tired when she leaves. While I clean up our mess I can hear her sweet voice in the emptiness of the house.

———

I've been in the midst of another slump for about a week. This one started a few days after the baby visited. These are the times when nothing in particular is wrong but I am depressed and upset from the moment I wake up. That is, if I sleep at all.

These spells used to torture me. I endure them now and focus on the fact that they always come to an end. Suicidal thoughts have become few and far between.

This morning I wake up after roughly two hours sleep. Once again, I fight off the temporary sadness and hopelessness I feel. I have long since stopped trying to figure this 'first thing in the morning' feeling. It is a complex, twisted mixture of emotional, mental and physical discomfort and pain.

I am careful to get dressed because it seems to help when I look better on the outside. I cry off and on for seemingly no reason, then decide to go shopping. I enjoy it more than I used to, even when I'm alone. But I have to go early to avoid the crowds.

It's later than I usually leave by the time I'm in the car. As I walk into the store, I notice there are other shoppers, though not enough to make me nervous. I shop stress free for about half an hour.

Coming out of the dressing room for the second time, I see that the store has become crowded. Immediately, my heart starts to race and my hands shake slightly. I am uncomfortable; I think everyone is looking at me, and not in a friendly way. I recognize the symptoms and begin wrapping up my shopping excursion. I know I need to go home now.

I deliberately make pleasant conversation with the

woman who checks me out. This is a trick I learned a couple of years ago. If I make sure the last encounter in a store is positive, I have a better chance of driving home in a more peaceful state of mind. Today the trick is not working.

I'm driving home wrapped in negativity. I decide to give it a run for its money. I'm going to fight hard, irregardless of the tears that start and stop at will. I'm a cornucopia of toxic emotions and severe allergy symptoms in this spring season. My contact lenses are tear-stained and blurry by the time I pull into my driveway ten minutes away.

You made it home, girl. Thank you Lord.

I still give myself a mental high five as I unlock the door.

By the time I take my purchases upstairs, I am calmer and excited to try on my new clothing. I think about how I overcame the urge to abandon my shopping cart and leave the store. I chalk this day up as a win.

———

I have been snappy with Kenneth the past few days. I think the crankiness is because I have not slept. He has done nothing unusual or inappropriate, I just feel like I want to be alone. I push him, and everyone else, away. When I'm like this he's all too happy to give me space as needed. *Could it be my attitude?*

I sit down to write about the events of the day. I

really don't want to write today, but I write anyway. Maybe one day someone will read this and can relate to it. When I stop, I have to admit that I enjoyed the act of writing about what goes on in a day in the life of a woman like me.

———

Today is Saturday, the day after my shopping trip. I have no real plans today except some writing and housework. Kenneth calls from work this morning.

"Good morning," he says cheerfully.

"Good morning. How is your day so far?" I respond.

"Not so good. My car stopped running as soon as I got here."

He goes on to tell me he will need a ride from work, which is about half hour drive from our home. I go into problem solving mode as he speaks.

His car will need to go in the shop. He will rent a car until it is repaired. Reluctantly, I agree to do the honors since he's at work. Already, I am uneasy because this task is unexpected. Most days my activities are planned in advance.

As it turns out, I have to rush to go rent the car because the company closes at noon on Saturdays. Since Kenneth gets off work at three this afternoon and works tomorrow, there's no other option.

I call for a car to pick me up since I can't leave my car

at the rental office. I manage to push past the anxiety of being in the automobile with a stranger, but I'm sitting mighty close to the passenger side door. I make it before closing, and then decide to take the car to Kenneth now, rather than pick him up when he gets off work. He can bring me back home and I can have the rest of the day in peace.

Forty five minutes later I am home and everything is fine. What I've done today is no big deal for most people, but for me it is another indication that I am making progress. I didn't let fear or nervousness paralyze me.

Of course, Kenneth could have gotten a friend or co-worker to help if I were not able to. But, as I do whenever I can, I wanted to push myself a little further. So I said yes, even though I felt uneasy and inconvenienced.

I am a little moody the rest of the day, which is usual whenever I have to change directions unexpectedly. Today I managed, alone, to navigate those changes and was rewarded with a positive outcome. Even with my mood and chaotic start of day, I know that I have turned a corner in the right direction.

It's the Wednesday before Easter and I have an appointment with Dr. Charles this afternoon. The purpose of the appointment is to assess how I am doing with my medications so that he can decide whether changes need to be made. I tell him about the continued insomnia and he increases medications for sleep.

I am glad to share with him that I see, for myself, the light at end of the proverbial tunnel. I've been hearing that I'm getting better from him and Dr. Olen for some time now. Although their prognoses always gave me hope, only recently have I actually believed that the worst would one day end.

The doctor is more than pleased with the news. He agrees with me and says he continues to see positive changes as time passes. He also cautions me not to push myself too much, to rest when I can, and not be hard on myself if I feel that my progress has slowed; which will most likely happen.

Over the next few days I think about a question that Dr. Charles asked when I told him I believed I was getting better.

"Sheila, what do you think is helping to contribute to your progress?"

I think it over briefly. "Having my family's love and support helps, coupled with the therapy sessions and the tools I'm given in order to be proactive in my healing."

Dr. Charles nods and I continue.

"I pray some too. And of course, my granddaughter is incentive for me to get better."

The mention of my granddaughter lights up my face. The doctor smiles in return.

As I sit here today, I contemplate a few of the positive things I have picked up on my path to wellbeing. I have embraced myself now more than ever. It is easier for me to protect and defend myself at all costs. I discover the possibility for PTSD to provide me with the opportunity to reach out beyond myself in the future..

I've learned more about myself in four years than I have in a lifetime. These years have made me more humble and patient. Hiding the real me in the secret shadows of fear and shame is over and done with, I've learned not to be afraid of a measure of transparency.

As it stands currently, I don't think I can say I am glad about what happened. But I do recognize the mercies I've been shown despite the misfortunes. And for that I thank the Lord.

Two years ago Sherry and her family moved a three hour drive sway from where I live. Easter will be celebrated at her house this year. I count the days. I am excited to see everyone. The last time we were together was at my home on Thanksgiving

As always, we receive a warm welcome when we arrive. There are about fifteen family members here, which include my three nieces and three grandnieces. Sherry has prepared a feast. We give thanks, then dig in. After taking plenty pictures, the day is spent listening to music, dancing and talking.

All too soon, as usual, it is nighttime and we must get back on the road.

I'm appreciative for another holiday with the people I love. When we get home, I'm thankful we did so safely. I am grateful that on this Easter Sunday the PTSD symptoms took a back seat.

19 LIFE GOES ON: I'M LEARNING TO MAKE LEMONADE

I remember how angry and disoriented I was when the world kept moving forward after my husband died. I would look around and see people going about their lives, unaware that the world lost one of the most wonderful men who ever existed, in my opinion.

I recall thinking that somehow time should stop to honor his memory. His accomplishments should be read aloud for all to hear. Birds should stop singing, seasons should cease to change, and criminals should repent of all wrongdoing forevermore.

I even asked God if the universe could be put on hold just long enough for me to catch my breath.

Probably because of my selfish motives for asking, God's answer was, "No."

I know that was His answer because time continues to march on without missing a beat. Such fantasies are the stuff fiction movies are made of.

The day William died time moved forward at the same pace as it always did and always will each day, no matter who dies. Bills came in the mail on time each month, I grew older, summer turned to fall, and people lived the lives they were given.

Immediately, I had to endure being in the midst of everyday people talking, laughing, arguing, and just living their normal lives. I am incapable of describing, in writing or speech, my loneliness during those first months after his death.

Eventually, I was forced to try to keep pace with the world around me or else languish in a miserable living death. I have no choice. The truth is that the world should not have to stop and honor my husband. I have the responsibility to honor his life and memory by living mine to the fullest.

Although the statement is noble and the motives sincere, I'm not naïve to the fact that to accomplish this is complex and difficult. For me it involves tolerating the instability of soaring to the highest of heights then plummeting to complete darkness, frequently on the same day or within the same hour.

I dig in, determined to ride it out when I can. And each time the gloom is a slightly lighter shade of black as I wait out the worst episodes.

I have moments, as Dr. Charles predicted, when think I should be further along. I express this sentiment to both doctors over the course of many sessions.

"What's been going on since the last session, Sheila?"

"Some days are real good. Then, without warning, I drop into darkness."

"Why are you sobbing, Sheila?"

"I feel like I'm sliding backwards and I should be further along."

"Sheila, the episodes are classic in patients with PTSD. Sometimes they occur for many years after a trauma. Their severity and number of episodes should decrease over time."

Dr. Olen reminds me to accept that the trauma was not as far in the past as I think it to be. She helps me to understand that I am punishing myself by being upset because I believe should be better, or "cured", by now.

I've expressed my fears, anger and other issues in my prayers, too. The spiritual aspect of my life plays an important role in maintaining my sanity and keeping me balanced.

I think of traveling this road like completing a jigsaw puzzle. The pieces in my puzzle include family and friends, God and His Word, my mental health care team, and me. The puzzle cannot be completed without all of the pieces. The finished picture will be a more fulfilling and productive life, which will evolve and change as the years go by.

I don't have to burden myself with waiting until I am completely "cured", whatever that means, to live better. The steady increase in the quality of my life makes me a winner at the gate.

I have found effective ways to handle stressful or upsetting situations. To even admit that I am stressed is a huge first step. I have to first accept that some things still make me afraid, uncomfortable, or sad.

Acceptance opens the door for me to address, in one way or another, what is going on and how it is affecting me.

There are times when addressing the issue means I simply recognize its existence. But by far the most constructive form of acceptance is when I go beyond recognition and am able to take action.

Action may involve an internal dialogue in which I tell myself over and over that I will get through whatever is happening. At times I go beyond affirmations to proactively solve a dilemma. I flip the scenario by doing or saying specific things which result in a more positive outcome.

———

In the next chapter are some precise examples of situations which have occurred in my life in the recent past. I have included them as examples of how I achieved better results by using the steps I've outlined above.

Their purpose is also to promote and encourage a habit of accepting when an adverse situation or circumstances exists, rather than hide from or ignore it. Only then can it be determined whether it poses a threat to peace, contentment, or health. If so, it is necessary to maintain an offensive posture and fight back in order to reduce or eliminate potentially negative effects.

20 CLOSING OPEN WOUNDS

The sudden shock of watching the toll that TEN took on William has made me extremely sensitive to certain things I see or hear that hardly bothered me before. I avoid watching gory movies or exposing myself to anything which depicts pain and suffering, violence, sadness, or death as much as absolutely possible.

This first story demonstrates that an unpleasant situation can still find you when you least expect it.

Kenneth, me, Kim, Michael, Trina, and the baby took a weekend trip to the Blue Mountains of Tennessee last spring. We drove through a severe thunderstorm on Friday evening and arrived at the cabin safely. The next day, as we were about to go into a museum, Michael stopped to open the little compact stroller he picked up for my granddaughter.

He was bending over the stroller, which was in the trunk of our rented minivan, using a knife to cut the packing straps. The rest of the group stood nearby in the parking lot. It was a struggle to cut through the hard plastic material.

I heard him curse. We looked in his direction and saw that he sliced the inside of his forearm; his flesh lay wide open. I knew the injury was severe, though Michael did not appear to be in much pain. The blood was so dark. *He's cut an artery.* My thoughts were mirrored by all of us.

At first I froze in place when I saw so much deep crimson blood with no warning. Fear iced over my heart. I did not want my panic to show.

Our little family group immediately went into action. Before I knew it, Kim and Kenneth had used my granddaughter's jacket and made a tight tourniquet on my son-in-law's arm.

Immediately, blood spread like wildfire, soaking the flannel material. Blood was everywhere. It plopped down onto the concrete, dripped in the van's trunk and bumper, and soaked the towels provided by museum employees. I heard Trina on the phone with the 911 operator.

"We're at the Hollywood Wax Museum. My brother-in-law has a really bad cut and needs help."

Later on, Trina told us the dispatcher asked how he was injured, which explained the next words I heard her say as she stood in the parking lot holding my granddaughter's hand.

"It is an accidental self inflicted knife wound. No crime has been committed."

Michael stabbed on purpose? I imagine law enforcement sees this type of violence all the time, so they had to ask. We waited on the steps of the museum. Basically, we were calm as we comforted each other and congratulated ourselves for not panicking.

Police and paramedics arrived and confirmed that the deep cut required attention at a medical facility. All of the responders were sincerely concerned, friendly, professional, and helpful.

While my son-in-law was in the ambulance being examined at the scene, two firefighters cleaned the thick blood from the van and the stroller, and then put powder on the ground to sop up the blood.

We got him to the hospital quickly. He needed about seven stitches inside and out of the wound for it to close properly. The doctor told him the cut was less than an inch from severing the nerve.

The sight of the huge volume of blood and the raw open wound was traumatic for each of us. With deliberate effort, I stayed as calm as possible and helped where I could. Kim thought quickly and took action even though she was afraid for her husband. Trina and Kenneth were brave soldiers who took up the slack wherever they were needed during the crisis.

After leaving the hospital my behavior was a little weird, and it showed. I was sure people were looking at me thinking: What a strange woman!

I say to the curious and the critical: Go ahead and label me as a strange woman. Just make sure you label me as an undefeated strange woman.

I prevailed by intentionally working to prevent the flashbacks which tried to creep in. I concentrated on thanking God that Michael didn't rapidly bleed out in that parking lot. Giving in to my symptoms would have taken the attention away from where it needed to be.

So what if, afterward, I had a nervous stomach and didn't want my picture taken with a Forrest Gump wax figure? (Yes, we did go back to the museum.)

We all decided to continue our weekend getaway, and that was a bona fide victory too. God answered prayer; Michael was fine.

Back at the cabin, Trina suggested that I put the experience in this book. We all agreed it was a good idea.

————

I call this one a "you can run but you can't hide…from God" story.

For the better part of my life I have found myself encouraging or counseling other women or girls. The hurting and wounded have been drawn to me as a listening ear, or for advice and comfort since I was a child. I'm fully aware that my ability and willingness to serve the wounded is a spiritual gift, not just my charming personality.

In fact, my plan was to start on the path to creating a ministry exclusively for hurting women. By the time William and I finished the ministry class, I was gladly taking calls day and night from women in Georgia as well as Michigan who were in a crisis of some sort, needed encouragement, or someone to just listen.

William's illness and death shut down those plans swiftly, like the darkness after the downward flick of a light switch. During those fateful three weeks, my love for ministering to others gradually faded, then died; probably around the time I left William's body in a casket beneath a green canopy on that hot summer day.

For years afterward I believed I would never be able to bear the burdens of others because my own were so great.

No doubt, if I had asked for the strength to help carry the weary load of the sorrows of other people, God would have granted my request. I didn't want to, though. At that time I could not see that I was surrounded by people with troubles of the same magnitude, and even greater, than mine. As I get better, I clearly see, and feel, the sorrows and suffering of others.

For a couple of years now, I have come across several women whom I never met who just begin to confide in me about some adversity they are going through. It happens when I'm running errands like grocery shopping, or having my car serviced.

One young woman is a manicurist in her early twenties. She was very friendly and sweet when we met the first time she did my nails.

As we made small talk I noticed that tears stood in her eyes whenever she looked up and made eye contact. Then she told me her husband died recently of cancer. She was not born in the United States and her parents still live in her home country.

I was given the strength to listen to her story and tell her that I am also a widow, though I didn't share the details of my loss. The conversation turned to God. She is a Buddhist, yet allowed me to share some Christian beliefs about how God comforts the hurting.

She showed me a note that another Christian woman gave her months ago. The note contained a scripture from the bible, John 3:16. She told me she keeps it in her drawer at the shop and reads it all of the time. The day I met her she said she was missing her mother very much. We reconnect each time I visit the nail shop and I make sure I give her an encouraging word.

I recall a time, not so long ago, when it was unbearable for me to hear sad stories, especially ending in death. But lately, when a person in pain is placed in my path, I don't usually avoid the interaction.

It was in God's plan for my life all along. The truth is that I have always loved to assist people or share whatever I have. He knew all along that helping others would be a powerful weapon to use in the battles I would face to save my life. Which is why I have never been able to put it down, whatever my circumstances.

———

This last story is not easy to write about, which is why I chose it over some of the stories I thought about inserting at this point in the book.

I was raised up by my mother and stepfather until his death in 2012. My biological father is still alive and well in his 80's. I saw him only a time or two in my childhood. We met again when Kim was born, and for some years afterward we saw one another regularly.

Since then we communicate sporadically at best for a number of reasons. However, he does call me when my mother tells him about a crisis I may be going through, like when my husband died.

Unmistakably, we do love one another but haven't had a consistent relationship in many years; mostly because of the hurt I harbored about the circumstances which caused the chasm between us. I admit I had been guarded with him rather than risk more hurt.

Many years ago I totally released the hurt and replaced it with acceptance of this destiny. I don't ask or pray for change of what has been decided in the situation. I'm content that at least we are always respectful and caring in our interactions with no ill will.

Our core issues will probably never be completely resolved. It's unlikely that we will have a close father and daughter relationship or see each other regularly. But I'm glad we are not estranged to the point we can't communicate at all, as I've seen with other families.

Once I accepted these things I knew it was possible that he and I could (and should) keep in touch regularly at the very least. He's my father and he gave me life. I get a lot of my traits, like dry sense of humor, uneven temperament, and money management skills from him.

For the past year or so he has been on my mind more, so I call him sometimes. The older I get the more I see how much I look and think like him. Through stuffy noses and runny eyes we laugh together that I have inherited severe allergies from him. I enjoy our short conversations and the taste of lemonade in my mouth when we hang up.

21 I'M STILL HERE: REFLECTIONS

One fond memory I have from grade school is the day the teacher spoke to the class about being the best we could be and the importance of making a positive mark in this world.

"Point your finger to the ceiling and jump up as high as you can," she instructed.

We all giggled and did as we were told. When we settled down, the teacher gave us something to think about when we got home.

"Boys and girls, you just left a mark in the universe with the tip of your finger. This mark will always be in the air; it will forever be proof you were here."

I don't recall the name of the teacher, or even the grade I was in at the time. But to this day I remember that gesture as though I performed it just this morning. For months afterward I thought about the exercise and lecture.

Fascinated, I pictured my little fingertip imprinted in the atmosphere as verification that I existed. It would stay there in place until the end of time, I imagined.

When I ponder over that incident from so long ago, I suppose the teacher started us on a path toward deeper thinking with regard to our existence and its purpose. Like millions of other children, as well as adults, I have wondered why I am here.

When I was in my early twenties, I took a photocopy of my hand with the copier at my place of employment. I won't forget my mother studying the copy with a somber look on her face when I showed it to her.

"What is it?" I asked.

"Your fingers stand out against the dark background as though you're saying, 'I'm here'."

At the time I laughed at her strong reaction to the picture, which she still has among her possessions.

Many years later, when my father died, I ran across the picture again. I stared at it and understood to some degree what my mother saw in its poignant image. It is my unique handprint. It is physical evidence that Sheila existed that day.

I'm sure every human being contemplates, analyzes, and then calculates their personal sum total, inside and out. Most likely, we still compare ourselves to others and try to guess whether our worth is greater. But our bottom line, so to speak, is as individual as our DNA.

As for me, I was always afraid to dig too deeply into who, what and why I am me. Maybe I was scared that my sum total was worthless, otherwise known as insecurity.

The trauma and subsequent therapy have pushed me to do so in recent years. I acknowledge, finally, what and who I am now and see myself as one of many other priceless gems whose value is determined by its existence.

Living among millions of people in the world, I am a

unique physical, mental, and spiritual being wrapped in the package that contains my body, mind, and spirit. Me.

Sometimes this awareness comes when I am going for a walk and happen to focus on my shadow that is beside or in front of me, depending on the sun's location. I think, *That's me on the ground.*

When I am away from home I take mental pictures of special moments or beautiful inanimate objects like trees or flowers. I save them in a sort of cerebral album and pull them out in times of stress. It's one of my coping mechanisms.

Other times, especially when I am stressed, I take the same mental photographs of the ugliest, most painful words or circumstances. They too, call out to me to look at them and repeatedly relive the memories.

Sometimes I do, but not as regularly and not for very long as I did a few years ago. But I own them, just like the images that are beautiful and positive. They're mine. And I can choose to do with them what I want. One day I will destroy them for good.

————

I feel humbled every time I stop and really think about how much people love me, and the influence I am honored to have on their lives. These thoughts are inspirational and a sure fire method for me to come from out of myself and concentrate outward, toward the important people and missions in my life.

I've been the person who hears compliments and accolades from others, but only allows them to flicker, and then mentally blow them out like candles on a birthday cake, without letting their warmth sink in. I'm getting better at letting the light of the successful me shine.

Life is a series of lessons to be learned. I am a student who is never too old for discovery. For example, I've found that many of the powerful toxic emotions I have now are actually the bigger, badder, and more dangerous grandchildren of feelings I remember having since I was a child.

The severity of the trauma with William, and so suddenly, was the food which fed them until they grew out of control and resulted in mental illness. It's just a theory of mine, I haven't conducted any reliable medical research on the subject, though I find that it does answer many of the questions I have about myself.

No matter, because the positive, constructive aspects of my character that I was born with, like intelligence, generosity, and humor are alive and well. They, too, have been nourished by the positive people and things in my life and thrived with the passage of time. My big heart, though wounded, is still open to give and receive love. The winner: Me.

One 'mark' of mine that still remains in the atmosphere is bravery. I can think back on hundreds of scenarios in which I flew in fearlessly where others dared not to venture, and not always toward something or someone that was good for me.

Currently, I push through boundaries which left me paralyzed a few short years ago, teeth grit from the uneasiness, but going in anyway. Like this book. The number and variety of attacks increase as I get closer to the end. I am determined not to give up. And I am grateful that I have supporters who carry my vision on their shoulders to keep it above water so that I can work to complete it.

The phrase "the bottom line" is used to indicate finality to a situation. As I write these words I realize I know longer believe there is a bottom line to anything or anyone.

People, places and things perpetually change due to time and circumstances. So I'll use the phrase, "what I know so far" to refer to my summation.

One thing I know so far is that I'm neither heroine nor villain. In my heart I'm one of the good guys, even when I fall short. I've had my fair share of mistakes and bad choices. And just as often I get it right.

I see my existence as a tapestry. Its threads and adornments are past and present people, places, and events. The finest of its threads is the dear man who inspired this book. He, for a time, unselfishly intertwined his wisdom, patience and love in my life.

Diamonds and other jewels array my tapestry. These priceless ornaments are my daughters, granddaughter, and other family members who are still here with me.

There are rips in the fabric, some tiny and others

huge. But they don't take away from its beauty or strength. Rather, they add character to the textile which is my life.

22 PRESENTLY

Post Traumatic Stress Disorder, with all of its disturbances, has not taken me away from this world physically or mentally. Instead, PTSD and I are partners in a dance in which I am gradually but surely taking the lead.

I am still active in my pursuit to emerge victorious every day. I'm definitely stronger and even more fearless than before. I face both the hard hits of life and the wonderful blessings equally.

I rarely have the intense suicidal thoughts I had several times a week for at least two years afterward. If I become very stressed and have a fleeting suicidal thought, I recognize it as merely a desire to remove myself from the stress or pain I'm feeling at that moment. I no longer have the desire to die.

I still have flashbacks sometimes in which I am actually in the hospital with William. I recall each conversation of the last week of his life. However, I'm so more adept at changing the course of my thoughts, which allows me to "leave the scene" and come back to the present faster than before.

As far as memories, both the good and bad remembrances are permanent fixtures in my mind. Not a day goes by that I don't miss William and the times we shared. Sometimes it hurts me to tears to remember his booming laugh, a movie he enjoyed, or his touch. Then there are times I can smile when something reminds me of him.

I dream about William once a week, at a minimum. Many of the dreams represent my conscience awareness that he's gone from me on earth forever. For instance, I dream that we are together and he gets lost. Hard as I try, I never find him. Or I dream that I am talking to him and his eyes won't meet mine.

The frightening nightmares about William's ruined face and body are fewer now. But for me, the real nightmares are when I dream he's fine, we are laughing and having a nice time together and the tragedy never occurred. And then I awake to a totally different reality.

I still have depression but, again, I fight to keep it from gaining control my life. I recognize when I am depressed and resist forcing myself out of it or pretending it doesn't exist. Instead, I take care of myself during these episodes and wait for them to pass. Sometimes I shamelessly pamper myself or someone else when I'm depressed; it distracts from the sadness.

Resting and sleep help relieve my depression. Talking with my therapist or family members lets me decompress, which relieves some of the depression sometimes. Other times I just need to be alone for a time.

Basically, I just feel my way through the episodes until I am better. And I always get better. Sometimes sooner, sometimes later.

I vigilantly watch for triggers of depression, just as I do with PTSD symptoms. The news is filled with reports of violence such as beating, murder rape, animal cruelty, etc. If I allow these reports to get in my head, they can make me depressed for several days. I keep exposure to a minimum. I get news updates from friends and family, and I check out news headlines regularly, making sure I limit my viewing time. The stories don't have as much impact upon me in smaller doses.

Sometimes I have outbursts of anger or plunge into deep sadness from unknown (or subconscious) triggers. I experience sudden terror on occasion from something as simple as not being able to find my keys to fear that a loved one is sick, harmed, or worse.

If I have to meet deadlines or tolerate time constraints I feel pressured. I still get anxious and stressed. I cannot sleep for days prior to an upcoming appointment or event because my mind obsesses about what I have to do. However, most of the time I do make it to where I need to go.

———

These days it is easier to recognize when I am at risk of continuing down an unhealthy mental path. I remove myself from the source of my discomfort and/or use one of several techniques to distract me or put me in a positive frame of mind.

I'm working on developing the responsible habit of taking time out when I reach my limit to avoid getting overwhelmed. Pushing myself past the point of exhaustion is a nasty habit I am determined to break.

I have been released from the burdensome guilt that I had for so long. Guilt is useless, harmful, and unbiblical. I've had unwarranted guilt from a child about one thing or another. But several issues related to William tormented me with guilt at one time. When he first got sick, I felt guilty that I did not take proper care of him in some manner. At the hospital I would sit at his bedside and think how angry his (deceased) mother would be that I allowed this to happen to her son.

When he died, I was haunted by memories of the times I was unkind to him or when we argued, as if ours were somehow worse than any other couple's disagreements. Guilt would creep in when I thought of times I was busy or tired when William wanted to go out for dinner or a movie. Silly things like that.

For a season I felt guilty for allowing another man in my life. I had to face the truth that William was not coming back, and my own truth that I am a woman who is used to and enjoys a committed relationship. And, of course, I had what is known as "survivor's guilt".

I now rest in the assurance that I was a good, loving, and faithful wife with faults like any other woman. I refuse to let guilt or useless, negative memories overshadow the wonderful blessing that was our marriage.

I would do anything to see him again, even for a moment. But what happened was not my fault. William's demise was neither my desire nor my call, it was a path created by the Eternal One. When I miss William's presence in my life, I find comfort in my belief that he is perfected for eternity.

I take life as it comes and try to keep myself from attempting to fix everything. And in the meantime, I'm happy to say that I'm successfully coping in spite of a form of mental illness which, sadly, has destroyed so many people.

I communicate with God on a more regular basis. When I am able, I pray at my lowest times and it gives me comfort and strength. More importantly, I also pray thanks to Him for the good in my life.

A few months ago I was writing and all at once felt His presence with me. It had been so long, but it was unmistakably Him. I went through the house praising Him for about an hour.

Overall, when I see myself in the mirror I like what I see - flaws, symptoms and all. For decades, even minor imperfections or mistakes made me feel ugly, stupid and ashamed. I think back now and sometimes I cry, thinking about all of the time and energy I spent in a futile attempt to be as close to perfect as possible.

I speak more openly and directly when I communicate with people, especially my family. It is taking some getting used to, for me and for them. By nature I'm the peacemaker, hesitant to hurt people's feelings, sometimes to my own detriment. But I'm in the fight for my life, you see. So, though feelings have been wounded on both sides at times, it is necessary for us all and essential for me. I am reassured they understand.

I don't look for praise or fear rejection with regard to this book. I'm clear that it will serve its intended purpose, whatever that may be. All I know is that it is intended for good, not harm. I'm released from the responsibility for, or expectation of, the predestined destiny of this tale.

Each day I get to live with a mind geared toward keeping the peace, helping others, and giving as well as receiving love because I am loved by Him. The alternative would have been to lose my mind or my life.

And what about the potential to help others in the process? Well, that's miracle and grace of God personified. In me.

———

Kenneth and I are still together. We have discussed marrying - some day. (That's the best time frame I can offer; I'm still a work in progress.)

I respect Kenneth because he wants to sink or swim based on his own merits. But at his core, where it really matters, he's very much the same as William when it comes to loving and caring about me. He has his own style and personality, which is as it should be, even when it seems to clash with mine. We're a solid older couple, complete with being set in our ways and getting on each other's nerves, while not being able to live without each other.

I/we have not chosen a permanent church, although we do visit different churches periodically. We pray together each day and share scriptures and our spiritual beliefs.

———

My mother decided she finally wanted to move to the South. We moved her here after a month of planning. She lives in a lovely, peaceful apartment complex about ten minutes away from my home.

Kim, Michael and the baby moved to Georgia about three years ago, they are a twenty minute drive from me. Trina lives about the same distance; she goes to school in the city where I live. It is going on ten years since we moved from Michigan. At last, my nearest and dearest are within reach and I'm pleased with this arrangement, to say the least.

23 POST TRAUMATIC STRESS DISORDER INFORMATION

The mental health condition Post Traumatic Stress Disorder (PTSD) is seen in people who have experienced or witnessed a traumatic event, or series of events. The exposure can lead to serious adverse effects. However, the cause of the condition and its severity is dependant upon the individual and the specific situation.[2]

Many years ago, PTSD was considered as a psychological condition which only combat veterans suffered due to the shock of their battlefield experiences. Currently, it is recognized as a condition which occurs both in and out of combat.

My diagnosis is a result of my close proximity to the sudden and extremely traumatic illness and subsequent death of my husband. Many other people around the world who have had similar experiences are treated for PTSD on a daily basis.

Military (combat and non combat) personnel comprise a large percentage of PTSD patients, as well as survivors of violence or the threat of violence, disaster victims, first responders, rescue personnel and caregivers,

---

[2] The National Institute of Mental Health lists specific incidents which can result in PTSD.
http://www.nimh.nih.gov/health/topics/post-traumatic-stress-disorder-ptsd/index.shtml

to name a few.

Most everyone on the planet has gone through a stressful or terrifying event or situation. It is a common reaction to be unable to function normally or bounce back quickly after such occurrences. However, such setbacks are not necessarily defined as Post Traumatic Stress Disorder, especially if the person is able to eventually get better on their own after some time has passed.

In most cases, PTSD symptoms increase and continue for months or years.[3] The symptoms become debilitating to the point they interfere with functionality. PTSD symptoms, on the whole, are prolonged and intense. Common Post Traumatic Stress Disorder symptoms include:

- Upsetting memories of the trauma which intrude upon thoughts on a recurrent basis.

- Continual distressing dreams related to the event.

- Flashbacks in which the trauma is relived as though happening again (different from memories).

- Very strong reactions (physical or mental) to

---

[3] Comprehensive PTSD information from the Mayo Clinic. http://www.mayoclinic.org/diseases-conditions/post-traumatic-stress-disorder/basics/definition/con-20022540?utm_source=Google&utm_medium=abstract&utm_content=Posttraumatic-stress-disorder&utm_campaign=Knowledge-panel

anything that reminds the person of what happened.

- Deliberately avoiding thoughts, discussion, places, people, or activities related to the trauma.

- Negative changes in emotions (such as anger and irritability).

- Negative thinking and moods, such as feeling numb, depressed, hopeless, or terrified.

- Many other symptoms including insomnia, being frightened easily, not being able to concentrate, always on guard, and guilt.

The variety of symptoms may be more intense during stressful times or when something triggers the memory of the trauma. The Mayo Clinic, Centers for Disease Control and Prevention (CDC), and National Institute of Mental Health are among the organizations that suggest that anyone who has the symptoms of PTSD which do not get better between one and three months after a traumatic event seek professional help immediately.

There is unlimited information and resources available for people with PTSD, depression, or other mental health conditions and for those that love and care for them. The American Red Cross, CDC, Anxiety Disorders Association of America (ADAA), PTSD Alliance and local mental health facilities are just a few options for where to find advice and assistance.[4]

The information contained in this book is not intended to diagnose or treat Post Traumatic Stress Disorder or any other mental or physical condition. It is solely share my experience and to inform readers about PTSD and give a list of some organizations where more information may be found.

Do no rely on this information as a source for any type of medical advice. It is imperative that you consult with a medical professional to diagnose and treat any mental or physical symptoms that you experience.

That said, I sincerely recognize that reaching out beyond your comfort zone can be painful, confusing and difficult. In my case, it became the difference between finding my way back or giving in to debilitation and potential death. You or your loved one may need a lot of help or a just a little. The key is to find out. Please do so for yourself and for those you love.

---

[4] cdc.gov, http://www.ptsdalliance.org, ptsd.org, http://www.adaa.org/index.cfm

AFTERWORD

PTSD and the Undefeated Me is a compilation of events in my personal life journey so far, from my point of view.

I hope that in this book readers will see themselves or someone they love, whoever they are and whatever state life finds them in at the present time. Perhaps a word or two from my tale will cause laughter or bring tears; emotions that can bring relief to the soul.

The book may inspire someone to take the first tiny step toward getting better, or provide awareness that there are those of us who walk around in complete disorder without it showing on the outside. PTSD can be undetectable and not easily recognized until a person is in crisis.

Millions of people self-depreciate, hide, fear, and exhibit other symptoms because of circumstances beyond their control due to PTSD. I stand with those who also stay strong in the fight to live productively and reach out to others.

I have benefited greatly from hearing the stories of other people who have triumphed through incredibly adverse circumstances. There are so many other brave and remarkable men and women in the world; their stories have kept me buoyed in some of my darkest hours. One way I am paying it forward is to share my story too.

I've come a long way and I am thrilled to give my status a grade of "thankfully improving" since my diagnosis. I have an even brighter future ahead. My needs and wants have been provided to me, along with a loving and supportive family that I cannot do without. If you know someone who is struggling, maybe you can be a part of their support team. It could mean the difference between their success and failure.

After changing the title of this book at least a dozen times, I decided on "The Undefeated Me", partly because undefeated means to overcome a battle, to prevail over and defeat an opponent, causing an adversary to become frustrated.

My wish is that your success meets mine and that you prevail in all that you do.

ACKNOWLEDGEMENTS

I give praise to the Almighty God and The Son, Jesus. Thank you for never leaving me even when I could not face You in my feeble mortality.

Love and thanks to my daughters. Your love and laughter kept me alive – even when you were not in my presence. I'm so grateful and forever proud of how you supported me, even while you endured your own pain. Remember that it is never too late to accomplish your goals as long as you are living.

Simply put: My whole heart and everything I have belongs to you –Love, Grammy

Hugs and kisses to my only sister and best friend. You tried so hard (and still do try) to make it better. Thank you for being there even when I couldn't see you because I was in such darkness. Much love and devotion.

Mother, I love you. Thank you for what you've given me to become the woman I am today. Your love of the Lord all of these years has inspired your entire family. Your strength is a legacy you have given us all. It is comforting to know you pray for me daily.

Thank you for all you did for us, JHB. We love and miss you.

I want to acknowledge my love and appreciation for my son-in-law. I have considered you my son since the day we met.

To my brother-in-law who is has been a solid, stable presence in this family for close to forty years. Thank you, my brother and friend.

Thank you, Hawk, for your constant support and great ideas. I appreciate your courage to challenge and love me at the same time.

Thank you to my professional and caring medical team.

I am sincerely thankful for each and every person who reads this book.

-Sheila Kay

SPECIAL THANKS

To The Gentleman

Thank you for keeping your promise to show the girls and me what a husband should be and for the sacrifices you made for us. You taught me by example how to live life without settling for anything or anyone less than I deserve.

I thank you also for sharing the deeper things of God with me regularly. Your faith and patience were admirable and it was my privilege to see them in action through you each day.

It is not possible for you to ever be forgotten. You live in the heart and mind of every person who knew you here on earth.

I am at a total loss to find words or the time to describe all that you were to us here on earth. You are forever "on the other side of this thing", having left this mortality for blissful eternity.

See you there.

ABOUT THE AUTHOR

 Sheila Kay is an editor, writer, and business owner. Among her interests are travel, cooking, reading, and charitable endeavors.

In addition to preparing for the release of her next book, Ms. Kay is in the process of forming a non profit organization which will provide resources, support, and job skills training to homeless Atlanta residents seeking to return to the workforce.

Her professional memberships include The American Society of Authors and Writers and The Nonfiction Authors Association.

PTSD AND THE UNDEFEATED ME

A Memoir

SHEILA KAY

https://www.facebook.com/AuthorSheilaKay

AristocratPublishing.com

Future Title from Aristocrat Publishing

CITY OF THE SOFT SPOKEN

By Sheila Kay

Set in the fictitious town of Chadwick, CT, *City of the Soft Spoken* is a mystery novel.

When unsolved crimes under mysterious circumstances plague a small town, only one man is willing to find out who or what is responsible. But not one of the city's strange residents is willing to cooperate with the investigation that will make the streets safe again.

Residents of the small community fiercely covet the deep dark secrets that have the potential destroy to everything and everyone within its city limits – and beyond.

Because in the City of the Soft Spoken, it just isn't safe to tell.

44779638R00108

Made in the USA
Charleston, SC
07 August 2015